1

TABLE OF CONTENTS

ELASTIC ATTITUDE 'EXPANDING YOUR POTENTIAL'

INTRODUCTION

A mentor of mine once said.....

"It takes all of us to make any one of us successful. When you develop a refined appreciation for the all us, it's what empowers any one of us to succeed".

Hi, I'm Craig White, a successful entrepreneur and proud father of two amazing and beautiful children; my girls, Isabella and Alana. Since becoming a father, I find myself even more dedicated to always being the best I can be. Ensuring I am creating an environment for them to think differently and to believe in themselves too. This true and powerful, emotional motivation only comes from within; it comes from your heart and your soul.

I am so excited to bring to you 'Elastic Attitude, Expanding Your Potential' program. It has taken years to cultivate and expand from the original back in 2012. I have so much appreciation for everyone who has helped to shape me over the years. For those of you that have made a difference both positively and those that have challenged me, I am forever grateful. To those of you that have loved, shared, inspired and believed in me from the very beginning, I thank you. You see in my opinion, we all have a responsibility to believe in others, to be the wind beneath their wings and empower them to leap, to fall and to fly. This program is about expanding your potential in every area of your life, so you can be the pebble of change, the ripple of influence and the leader of excellence. I thank you for your impact and I challenge you to impact the world, our world, in the most positive of ways each and every day.

So let's get straight to the point; you're already here because you are hungry for change. You clearly want to expand your potential and the opportunities that lie within you, around you and before you. As a human being you are designed to change, develop and grow; it's in your DNA. Ultimately you must focus on consistent and never-ending improvement through developing new skills. You will find this program is far from just the typical sharpening of the axe tool. This program will expand your potential, shift your mindset and stretch your beliefs.

As a successful entrepreneur with a Passion To Succeed and a desire to contribute, you must know that I am personally dedicated to make a difference. My purpose is to empower people to live a more fruitful life and to be the greatest version of themselves. People just like YOU that have a hunger for personal growth, a desire to change and that passion to succeed too.

So who am I??

I discovered recently and I would like to share with you 'I Am', two of the most powerful words in the English vocabulary.

'I' encompasses one of the most powerful and intimate sources of self-acknowledgement.

'AM' accompanying 'I' side by side, ensures that together both words will act as a statement that embodies personal strength and purpose.

Any word that you place after these two words, act as a declaration of truth, impacting your subconscious and developing stronger beliefs.

Using these two words 'I AM', you can affirm it to yourself every day, continuing to expand your own potential and strength. You are everything you dream of being. If it is inside you, if you can think it, if you can see it, you can 100% achieve it. You already 'are' and you can say:

- I am strong.
- I am dedicated to succeed.
- I am here to make a difference and contribute.
- I am ready to expand my potential.

Personally I am here to impact the world with my passion for people, my passion to succeed and my mission to influence YOU to be the most amazing version you choose to be.

When I look back from an early age I loved to lead; it was clear I enjoyed positively influencing others. Now it is of no surprise to me. that many years ago I set what would be deemed an audacious goal at the time. My ambition was to become good enough to create an empowering audio program and donate all proceeds to charity. I used 'I AM' and still do to this day, to affirm ability and confidence in all I do; you should too.

Through my personal development journey I was inspired to achieve and I aspired to grow to that level of ability, to impact and empower others too. Back in 2012, with a little help from my friends, I was really proud to have been able to do exactly that and donate over £8,000 to the Children of Barnardo's at Christmas. The audio program was called 'Elastic Attitude'. Back then, and still to this day, I am dedicated to be someone who can continuously learn and study success, allowing me to make a difference and contribute to other people's journeys too. I believe whole heartedly;

"What is the use of money and knowledge if you are unable to give it away?"

This personal mission of mine remains as strong as ever and it is why I now bring to you an expanded version of Elastic Attitude, giving you more depth of development. The knowledge, principles and areas of focus in this new program will really raise your game and take you to the next level. We are going to:

- Get you thinking differently, shifting your mindset to that of a super achiever.
- Awaken that sleeping power to live out who you truly are in line with your own personal truths.
- Enable you to create more certainty and confidence in your own ability and the possibilities before you.

- Help you unleash that passion and power that everyone has within them. To learn, develop and impact this world for the greater good of one and all.

You are going to discover and learn some life changing insights and philosophies. Ones that linked with the correct action steps in this program, will give you your own personal road map and blueprint to succeed. Your story and your journey of growth starts today. I hope you are as committed as I, and as ready as I, to raise your game and expand your ability to contribute with confidence, reaching new heights in all you do.

ABOUT THE AUTHOR

My story is far from a 'rags to riches' story. It is a story of personal growth, personal development and a passion to be more, to achieve more. I was born into an amazing environment with two positive, dedicated and hard working parents. As environments go, I had it great. I was challenged to compete. I was believed in and raised to believe that I was good enough in all I did. My parents taught me some core values, values of contribution, teamwork and discipline that really shaped me and continue to do so today.

At school I was always positive and like everyone, I excelled at what I loved and did it to the best of my abilities. Like most young lads, my ambition was to play football for my team, Liverpool FC. I was playing football at every opportunity, modelling myself on the great footballers of the time, Ian Rush, John Barnes and Craig Johnson, to name a few. During these years I was propelled into being a young entrepreneur through hearing and learning of the entrepreneurial stories of my family. It is all about environment, modelling and association right?

The most impactful one, the story that gave me a light bulb moment was about my grandad, Ronnie Harris. My grandad was a family butcher, living above the shop in Upton on the

Wirral in the UK. I was told this story of how my grandad and his best friend at the time, who I believe was also a family butcher, had created and started a football pools on the side of their traditional businesses. For my grandad, it gave him so much enjoyment and was a lot of fun because it combined 2 of his passions in life. He loved football, was an avid fan and also enjoyed to have a bet, so it perfectly suited him and I am guessing was an ease to do. When you love what you do, it's relatively easy in my opinion.

As the football pools developed and continued to grow with popularity, it became more demanding and my grandad decided it was taking up too much of his family time, so he simply handed it over to his good friend to run by himself. However, his good friend really didn't want to run it without him, so he passed it onto his father to run, who then gave it to a gentlemen called Cecil Moore. It was great fun while it lasted, both my grandad and his friend had enjoyed the fun it bought to them however, it just became bigger than they wanted. Interestingly, with its new owner it continued to grow and it became one of the biggest football pools in the UK. Till the day my grandad passed, and even beyond, my Nan, Violet Harris never let him forget he'd given away such a successful business. Though he was happy with his decision as it enabled him to be the family man he chose to be, his legacy continues today.

So the light switched on and my entrepreneurial journey started at age 14. I began a football pools at school, which was a lot of fun and a nice little earner until thwarted by the headmaster of my school. Who would of thought that gambling and showing business acumen would be looked down upon?

My mind was open, and it was as though I was attracting entrepreneurial opportunities. I was climbing around the loft of our family home and I discovered this weird looking gun contraption. It was an ear piercing gun of my dad's from when my parents ran a hairdressers in London. Another entrepreneurial story graced my environment and so began my second little business.

I was piercing ears during school break times; "£1 an ear, bring your own earring". This was a fantastic success until again I was reprimanded for my money making mindset. After again calling my parents into school for my behaviour to be discussed, my mum later told me how proud she was of me for having the guts and insight to try these businesses. Yet she was very clear that I must respect the rules of the school and to never do it again during school time. To be honest it took the challenge and excitement away, not to mention the mass market I had at such a large school. I believe it was around then, with my new found hunger for earning an income, that I got my first job as a pot wash, yet now I was being paid by the hour. Little did I know back then, how I was exchanging my time for money, helping someone else achieve their dreams while they paid me what they thought I was worth.

A couple of years later, like most people I guess, I left school and went into further education to realise that I had no desire to sit in a classroom anymore. I wanted to be out in the world making money and experiencing life. The dreams I had as a child had already started to fade away into the distance, becoming a pipe dream, the life that was for other people. Have you ever felt like this too?

"The dreams we have as children fade away."

I was going from job to job, looking for something that I really enjoyed and wanted to do. The challenge was gaining that so called 'necessary experience' every desirable position required. Finding something that energised me, even interested me, was proving to be a rather large issue. With my income never exceeding £15,000 per annum, the childhood dream of driving a black Porsche 911, living in a big house and having that lifestyle dreams are made of, continued to fade away into the distance.

Looking back at those early days of employment, I had no particular vision for my future. I had no clue what I really wanted to do. Even after my entrepreneurial start, I had been conditioned and sucked into the employment trap. No wonder the dreams I had became exactly that, just a dream, a wish even, and I had no genie in a magic lamp. What I did have, was a magic work ethic. I possessed what I now see as a 'sweat equity mindset.'

I was willing, and still am today, to work hard and burn that midnight oil and leave my mark on the playing field so to speak. I had three jobs at age 16/17. I was hungry. I had a full time job selling fax paper, of which from memory I am pretty sure I sold none! Then I had 2 part time jobs just to fund my desired lifestyle, however I actually found I had no time to do anything. I am sure you will agree this is common in the employment world today, for most men and women. You either have little income left each month and plenty of time, or in comparison you have a superb salary and no time to enjoy the fruits of your labour. I am so pleased I had been conditioned by my parents to never settle for anything less than what made me feel happy and fulfilled, again I have my mum to thank for some sound advice;

"Son, if you dislike what you are doing, stop doing it and go find something that makes you happy."

You may be wondering, why am I telling you all of this? Too many people get stuck in a rut and spend their life settling for second best, even doing things that negatively affect who they are. Why? Because it's easy. No. Believe me, it's tough spending your days unhappy, unfulfilled and under-valued.

I am sharing this small snippet of my journey with you because I believe I am no different to the rest. What I also believe is, you have the ability to feel fulfilled and be successful, it is in your DNA, every one of you. This program will enable you to tap into the possibilities that are within you and allow you to evolve, to grow, to change, and awaken the success that lies within.

I have been broke, suffered great loss, and maybe like you, I have been through struggles. I've faced adversity and been drowning in a sea of debt, shackled by the conformity of society. I would like to challenge you to break free, to open your eyes and to stretch yourself. Today you are in the Age of the Entrepreneur. Today is the day that you can embrace greatness and change.

"How we change is how we succeed."

I believe Elastic Attitude is going to be your 'catalyst for change.' It will be the shining light to lead you, to help you cultivate yourself into becoming unstoppable. You are here on this program, on this page of your life because you're hungry for more. You must be ready to expand your potential and remove the chains that have held you back. The ambition I have always had with Elastic Attitude is to help you remove this disease of complacency that spreads throughout the world; to help you build better relationships and to make more money.

I will only be sharing with you what I have learned and what I have done that has allowed me the freedom to live on my terms. Over the next 5 chapters I am excited to share with you strategies, philosophies and areas of focus that have enabled me to build a £35 million network marketing business, a successful property portfolio and an exciting personal development platform. This is all great, but I believe it is just the beginning, and today is the beginning of our journey together.

"From every beginning, can come great results."

I challenge you to make the decision, to put your best foot forward and commence a new journey, to develop new skills and new beliefs. I would like you to understand one thing before we get started on this exciting journey together. I personally believe this to be a major contributing factor to your achievement:

"Your Personal Passion To Succeed."

When you are passionate about something, you can become excellent at it. Passion is the fuel to your personal bank of energy and motivation, it is what will allow you to become a super achiever in the areas of life that you are passionate about.

I am very honoured and grateful that you have chosen to develop new skills and further your personal growth with this program. In doing so you give me purpose and it is a pleasure to contribute to you and serve you on your journey. I hope Elastic Attitude truly expands your potential and takes you to the next level. I am going to share with you everything I have in this program; everything in my heart and soul that continues to serve me well. The first chapter is about shifting your mindset, being elastic and pushing to your limits.

Be driven by your own purpose, your truth, your love and passion for what you do.

Thank you, and enjoy the program.

Craig.

CHAPTER 1 - BEING ELASTIC

'You will never know your limits until you push yourself to them'

Many years ago a friend and colleague of mine told me:

"People are like elastic bands. To be successful, one must be stretched."

Fascinating really, when you consider how many elastic bands around the world are sat on the shelf, unfulfilled, unused, waiting to be purchased and for someone's hands to use them for the purpose they were made. Are you thinking what I am thinking? Finger guns and giant band balls! I guess us guys never grow up hey.

Consider for a moment, how many unfulfilled human beings around the globe today, are sat waiting for, even relying on someone else to lead them, shape them and help them unleash their given potential? I imagine so many people, maybe even you until now, are sat on the shelf watching life drift by. How many times have you heard:

- You only live once.
- One life, one chance.
- Life is no dress rehearsal.

Life is far from a spectator sport, it's a game to get involved in, to play your hand, live your life and be the best you can be. Every one of you is a leader of your own destiny, now it's time to take control of your life.

"A leader of one is a leader of many, if you're unable to lead one you'll never lead any."

I believe leadership is present in all you do as an individual, you are the creator of your own environment, which in turn influences others. Everyone of you has a leadership responsibility, a responsibility to contribute, to stop relying on others and to take ownership of your own actions and decisions. You are always leading the way for someone to follow in some way shape or form and people will always pay more attention to what you do rather than what you say. Become the leader you seek through the inspiration around you and inside you. Generally you will find that people are compelled into action through inspiration or even desperation. You have a trigger point that encourages you to act; an emotional and motivational connection; a point when the switch switches in your mind, and you discover

21

that inner motivation. It has always been there, you just need that one moment in time, that emotional connection that triggers you to think and to act differently.

Surely, you have heard "When the student is ready, the teacher appears". Something will always trigger your mind and imagination to act in line with your beliefs and personal desires, even inspiring you out of your self-imposed comfort zone. My personal trigger point was reading a marketing flyer promoting an audio program;

"Awaken the Giant Within" By Anthony Robbins.

It captivated me. I was ready. Reading this small leaflet inspired me to believe I had the potential to awaken my own sleeping giant. However, I instantly made a decision that I had to listen to this audio first, to see if I really had it, if I really could unleash my apparent 'inner power.'

The challenge I had was quite simple, I was broke. I lived with my parents and although I had amazing family and friends; I just had a tonne of debt. My solution, albeit a shameful one, was to secretly borrow my father's credit card. Interestingly he later found out while I was sharing this exact story on stage in front of 450+ attendees a few years ago. Thankfully, he was pleased that this had set me 'on my way', let's just say. I am always buying my dad a drink on beaches all over the world!

I was absolutely buzzing from the high energy, passion and enthusiasm for success this guy possessed through the audio program. It literally unleashed a power of certainty. I started believing in the dreams that had faded away almost instantly and I had this confidence to pursue them. This was my 'personal catalyst for change', it was from that day on that I consciously changed my environment and started to cultivate a mindset and a way of thinking that would allow me to grow, becoming worthy of the success I craved.

Throughout this chapter I want to share with you how you can create new habits, forming new patterns and pathways in your mind to develop your mindset to become different to the masses. These simple yet impactful philosophies will help you embrace the age of the entrepreneur and overcome the common challenges every entrepreneur faces. Prevention is far better than a cure and it is essential you avoid getting lost into entrepreneurial nothingness. This is when the initial energy and excitement for something new fades away. It's where a new entrepreneur gets lost in the fog, confused in which direction they should go and slowly retracts back into a comfort zone where failure is certain.

This whole program, piece by piece, step by step, will develop the foundations for you to overcome any obstacle, every challenge that comes your way, with a startling heroism and confidence to excel. Lack of confidence is so often something many people can hide behind. Everyone has the moments of lost confidence, yet when you have positioned yourself in the right environment, there is no genuine reason for this to hold you back. When the desire is strong and we will discuss this throughout the program, confidence never comes into it as we are unconsciously driven to do whatever is needed to be done. Confidence comes from doing.

"Do the thing and gain the power."

When your personal confidence challenges you, I would like you to adopt this simple thought process. Think of how you can focus on contribution. From contribution, grows confidence. Focus on giving your positive input. Focus on activity and contribution first. Have a little blind faith and just do it. Why? Because you can!

So are you ready to expand your potential?

Let me share with you a simple and essential foundational belief, that I challenge you to adopt today as a truth, with all your soul;

"If someone else can do it, then so can you."

This simple belief sits at the foundation of every great achievement and every positive contribution that lay before you. The challenge is, Your Mind.

The way you think can immediately determine if you will or if you will not. Simply because you may feel you're unable to do that now, you may feel you are not ready or have never done it before. Your life is a journey, step by step block by block you can learn 'how' and develop the skills both mentally and physically to do anything someone else has. It's your desire, rather than your ability that'll determine your results.

Regardless of where you are right now, start with what you have and better skills will be found and cultivated along the way. If someone else can, so can you. You have so much evidence all around you that shows this to be true. Over the years so many individuals have modelled themselves on other people's successes. If you model yourself on those that can, those that do and those that have, you are stepping in the right direction too. We will discuss this more later however, it is in your DNA. It is an instinctive human behaviour to naturally copy and duplicate others in all we do. So if you really want to do something, learn and/or achieve something new that you have seen others do however big or small, you can 100% learn how to achieve and do it also.

So let's for a moment, consider what characteristics you believe are worth modelling and adopting as your own. What would you believe to be the top 7 characteristics, attitudes and habits of a successful entrepreneur, athlete, parent, leader in their field? Write down what you consider to be your personal top 7 traits of those that inspire you:

1.

2.

3.

4.

5.

6.

7.

Every characteristic is learnable and duplicatable. Have a look for a moment and consider what characteristics you feel are your strengths and which ones you would like to develop. You will already bring your own strengths to the party so to speak, and what's interesting is all characteristics can be acquired through focus, association and a commitment to learn, develop and change.

Spend a moment and just measure yourself on a scale of 1 to 10; 1 being poor and 10 being a strong characteristic. It's important to understand, what you avoid measuring, you'll never grow, and like every journey you need a starting point, so write down beside each trait your current grade so to speak. Once you have positioned yourself with a starting point, you can develop a road map from A to B. So ensure that you have noted where you think you are at the moment, then I would suggest you first work through this program and then revisit these points to developing your road map of personal growth. It is also wise to enlist the support and guidance of a mentor or a coach. If you are yet to connect to my Passion To Succeed Facebook page, check it out today, www.facebook.com/Passion2Succeed Once you are connected, search for a live training 'Creating Your Blueprint'. This is a training I do every 90 days to help our community focus on what's required for continued success and personal growth in all areas of life.

For now, let's immediately take this to the next level. I would like you to spend a few moments on each of the 7 characteristics you have noted. Focus on one at a time and consider someone you know, even a mentor to you or inspiration from afar that displays this character strength. What is it you see and feel about them that highlights this particular strength? Why is it you believe they possess this strength and how do they show this to you? Write it down beside your noted traits. Take the time now, before you move on, it is essential you notice the detail that you find attractive in each of these 7 traits.

So let's be straight, if, like I would have done 10 years ago, you have jumped this section thinking I'll do it later, STOP! How we change is how we succeed and action is the glue to all success. If you truly wish to expand your potential, it's time to do the things that others never do. Complete the tasks needed. It's in these moments when no one else is watching, where the magic happens, so sit down and get involved in creating lasting and tangible change today.

We have now established a characteristic starting point for you. We have also considered mentors and inspirations and you have developed an idea of the strengths they possess that you deem both fascinating and aspirational. The next step in this process is to develop your own action plan to mirror these characteristics, simple step by step points to lead you to develop the strengths and traits of those that inspire you. Why? Because every skill can be acquired with a strong enough desire and a personal road map to make it happen.

So your task right now in theory, is quite simple, although occasionally it can be a challenge to highlight our own personal areas of focus. This is where your mentor and coach can be of great assistance to help you with a fresh set of eyes. Though for now, let's dive right in.

What I would like you to do is spend a few moments on each characteristic and write some points, even a paragraph, whatever suits you best, in the section below. Consider:

- What do you feel you need to mirror?
- What are your areas of focus?
- What action points can help you develop that skill/trait?

What skills do you need to cultivate alongside your existing strengths, to grow, to become more and to be able to give more in your arena? Remember, you are always developing anyway, now you are taking control in choosing your own path through calculating the steps to mirror and model others on purpose. For example, as we discussed earlier:

To gain more confidence, focus on contribution; giving first and taking action. Do the thing and gain the power.

It's fascinating how having guided direction, focus and accountability can bring out the answers and knowledge with clarity, we sometimes never knew we possessed.

1.

2.

3.

4.

5.

6.

7.

We have already established you are here on this page of your life, reading these or even listening to the audio because you want more out of you; you want more out of life. It is clear to me that you wish to become more, give more and achieve more. Why else would you be on a journey of personal growth and on this program? I believe there will be things you wish to share, see and feel in your life that have the power to give you the feeling of fulfilment.

If you consider for a moment the areas of focus you set out to personally cultivate your skills and develop new strengths; to succeed you must focus on:

- The CHOICE to take the CHANCE and make the CHANGE.
- Constant and never ending personal development.
- A service to many; positively influencing others.
- Giving value without need of compensation.

For things to change we must change. Remember, how you change is ultimately how you will succeed. We do live in a world of abundance, where anything is possible for those that believe it to be so, if at first you just believe. This world of ours has a unique way of giving you exactly what you ask for in alignment with what you desire and deserve. There are three particular points; ways of being, a way of thinking and living an abundant, fun-fueled life of friendship and adventure. This is where I'd like to introduce what I call my three E's;

EXCITEMENT

ENERGY

EXPECTATION

Would you agree with me, being excited is essential to live an enjoyable life? That feeling you get when you're excited to see someone, excited to do something new, that nervous energy even, that shines through in all you do. Seeing other people excited is uplifting, inspiring and warming. You must have heard in your time, "It's not what we say it's how we say it." It's the excitement in your voice that captures people's attention. Excitement is everything.

Where does this excitement come from? It comes from being in line with your truths. It shows itself when you're doing something you love and even doing something for someone you love. It's that childlike wonder for life, learning and doing new things. Excitement comes when you wake up every day, loving what you do and you fall in love with being alive. Your life source should never be dulled. The energy you have when you are congruent to what excites you; when you are in an empowering environment of love, care and belief. Energy shines from the inside out. It shines through your eyes and brings a passion to your world around you. Everyone has the ability to get up, get busy and get in motion. Through motion comes further motivation. Everything is in energy. It's the source of life and your ability to be the greatest version of you. When you find certainty and clarity, it brings a belief and an energy. You must understand;

"You carry a lot of power when you totally understand and believe."

34

You may not always get what you want, yet you tend to get exactly what you expect. It's in your DNA to live a life of greatness. Start expecting only the very best for you and your life. It's ok to have high expectations. Expect and believe in the possibilities. You'll naturally attract positive outcomes; the outcome you expect and desire. Believe in greatness; contribute greatness and embrace all that comes your way with a positive expectation. Over the years some people have questioned my sanity, my thinking and my beliefs. "Here's Craig and his positive bubble, this crazy mindset and belief system!" Well, I have made my way through life implementing all you will learn in Elastic Attitude. You and I notice and observe things that are relevant to our beliefs. My awareness is in the possibilities and in positive expectations. I see the positives and I have trained my mind to see the greatness in everything. You can too.

This is how I choose to live my life. It's how I parent my children. It's how I coach and mentor my colleagues to be the very best they can be too. It hasn't always been this way. It is hard to be excited, energetic and enthusiastic when your best friend loses his life. The world closes in on you through the emotions of loss and life being unfair, it seems as though everything is against you. Your energy is sapped, it's easy to then start expecting and creating a life of loss, pain and mediocrity.

"Where attention goes energy flows. What you give energy to, you give life to."

Still to this day I feel the loss of my friend. However, I choose Yes. I choose to be inspired by our friendship, a friendship of adventure, trying new things, giving everything our best shot, and believing in our dreams. This loss was many years ago, yet I made a decision weeks later to live my life to the full and to continue to strive like we'd always done. Through every loss we find strength. Thank you Jamie for being the one that continues to inspire me to remain excited about life and expect only the best. It was famously said by the great Jim Rohn;

"The same wind blows on us all. It's how we choose to set the sail that determines our direction."

Within my Driven By Passion 7 week coaching program, one of the areas we focus on is;

The Environment

The environment we have found ourselves in and/or choose to put ourselves in, is what will ultimately shape our beliefs, actions and results. We are in a social and economic environment that favours the brave. We're in the infancy of the entrepreneurial age. In the future I believe that masses will be self-employed, yet right now society is failing to adapt. Just about everyone in the advance economy will be self-employed, yet we are still educated to get a job.

Let's go back in time, over 150 years to when 10% of the world found itself employed and the remaining 90% self-employed. Right now it is completely opposite, yet there is a shift. More and more people are realising they are under-valued, under-paid and under-appreciated. There is no longer such a thing as a job for life. Job security is a thing of the past. It is time to educate yourself; be adaptive; the better you can adjust, the better your outcome and that of our future society. It's time for change; to at first become uncomfortable and have the guts to make the change and join the wave of people around the globe becoming a part of this entrepreneurial wave; an age that is bringing back the passions that lie hidden within so many. A time where individuals can take back their own security in today's ever changing market. Yes, you must make a shift in the way you think; you must develop new skills, make new choices, take risks and push yourself that little bit more. Success lies when you stretch, when you push to the finish line:

Persevere

Until

Success

Happens

The opportunity, your opportunity to succeed in today's market is stronger than ever. Remember this, live by this, and strive with this understanding:

- SUCCESS LOVES URGENCY
- SUCCESS LOVES MASSIVE ACTION
- SUCCESS LOVES SPEED
- SUCCESS LOVES CONSISTENCY
- SUCCESS LOVES AND WANTS YOU TOO

Success in all areas of life comes to those that understand it's the burn that produces the results; it's that sweat equity. I believe you already have the ability, the potential and the power within you to do new things, make new choices and take the right steps in order to succeed in your arena. However, what often prevents people from an achievement is the "I can't, I'm not worthy, it's ok for them" self-talk. Everyone has this negative self-talk at some point in their lives. It's what you say to yourself that truly matters.

"The extra mile is between the ears."

It's what you believe to be possible that truly allows you to unleash that inner potential. I am sure you will agree, you are where you are today because of your choices and decisions of the past. So surely, your future will be shaped by your choices and decisions of today. What you may find quite scary is that most of your daily choices and therefore actions are made unconsciously by what Tony Robbins calls your "Executive Secretary." An executive secretary, I was over the moon when I discovered this, I had always wanted my own personal assistant. Though to then discover that everyone has an internal secretary so to speak, that makes most of your decisions automatically on your behalf, was a little scary to say the least. Interestingly, like most things, once you have this awareness you can learn to influence and control what is being done automatically for you. This executive secretary is actually called 'RAS.'

RETICULAR ACTIVATING SYSTEM

Confusing right? Not really. Basically your Reticular Activating System is a group of nerves in your brainstem that filters out unnecessary information and lets the important stuff get through. As we all know, our brains are incredible, they sift through billions of pieces of data. Basically your RAS will take what you focus on and it creates a filter that will only present the information that it believes to be important to you, like your name, or when you learn a new word, then you start to hear it all the time; it's your RAS in action. However, I prefer 'Executive Secretary' it has an air of success about it.

So let's consider this in simple terms, your executive secretary controls what information is presented to you, along with unconsciously making your choices, defined by your habits, the patterns of your life and through the routines that typically create your days. You are making choices and decisions, made unconsciously because that's how you always do it. It's comfortable for you, it's even easy. You could say your executive secretary protects you from failure, maybe even prevents you from growing, expanding and stretching to the next level. You can also make a decision that can seem insignificant in the moments of the day, when no one else is watching and you ask yourself:

Should I?

Can I?

Well, I personally believe, providing it's in line with creating your destiny, achieving your daily goals and in the greater good of one and all, this is when you must turn your 'Should I's', and 'Can I's' into 'I MUSTS.' This is where you consciously shift the way you think and what you give focus to, in turn re-training your executive secretary to new levels of greatness.

"Where attention goes, energy flows and where energy flows life grows."

Be sure to seek the positive paradigms; that shift in thinking, that awareness that sees the sunshine rather than the clouds of doubt. It starts in those small moments of decision when no one else is watching. Be aware of making the right decisions in line with your ambitions and desired outcome. Create a trigger in your mind to ask yourself:

"Is what I am doing right now, taking me towards or further away from my goals and targets?"

This action and resulting decisions can seem insignificant in the moment, yet compounded over time can produce phenomenal results, while training your executive secretary to be onside. This will result in fuelling your desire to strive more and succeed. Success isn't seen in these moments, however, it's in these moments when you choose to act in line with your goals, when it's just you and the man in the mirror saying 'yes' to your ambitions and turning them should I's into I musts. By the end of this program you will have your RAS onside and trained for exceptional success.

Let's review for a moment.

So the decisions in the moment, the sacrifices you make and the actions you take when no one else is watching, will determine your growth. It's in these moments where you win or lose. It's these moments when your goals, your why power and your emotional driving force, show up or shut up. Through your thoughts, you create new habits, cultivating new pathways and an 'I Can' belief system. Let me share something with you that I feel is relevant. I picked this up along the way on my journey to today. It's entitled:

BE MINDFUL OF YOUR THOUGHTS

Be mindful of your thoughts; your thoughts become words

Be mindful of your words; your words become your actions

Be mindful of your actions; your actions become your habits

Be mindful of your habits; your habits become your character

Be mindful of your character; your character shapes your destiny

Everything we will do together through this program is to shape a winning mentality. You can change the way you think and the way you act. You can learn to consistently make the correct and empowering choices, however you must have this unshakeable self-motivation, that passion to succeed that makes you unstoppable. In order to really raise the bar, to succeed in all you do, you must have that burning desire, that desire to do the things that others will not do.

I would like to share a story with you that really impacted me. It's from a great book called;

Chicken Soup for the Mother Soul by Jack Canfield and Mark Victor Hansen.

It's called;
Moving Mountains

There were two warring tribes in the Andes, one that lived in the lowlands and the other tribe lived in the mountains. The mountain people invaded the lowlanders village one day, and as part of their plundering of the people, they kidnapped a baby from one of the lowlander family's and took the infant with them back up into the mountains.

The lowlanders didn't know how to climb the mountain. They had no idea of any of the trails the mountain people used. They didn't even know where in the mountains they would find these savages or even how they would track them on the steep terrain.

Even so, they sent out their best party of fighting men to climb the mountain and bring the family's baby back home.

The men tried first one method of climbing and then another. They tried one trail and then another. However even after several days of effort they had climbed only a few hundred feet. Feeling hopeless and helpless, the lowlander men decided the cause was lost, and they prepared to return to their village below.

As they were packing their gear for the descent, they saw the baby's mother walking toward them. They realised that she was coming down the mountain, the same mountain that they hadn't figured how to climb. And then they saw that she had a baby strapped to her back. How could that be though? One man greeted her and said "We couldn't climb this mountain. How did you do this when we, the strongest and most able men of the village could not do it?"

The mother simply shrugged her shoulders and said; "It wasn't your baby."

What an amazing and uplifting story, gets me emotional, charged and even brings a tear to my eye. You see, when YOUR REASON WHY is big enough, when it's strong enough, when it pulls on your inner passion, you are motivated and powered through love to do the things that others cannot and will not do.

Self-motivation is an essential element to your success, and is triggered by your internal, emotional driving force. This emotional strength is something many people never really tap into or even spend the time discovering their truth. It's a strength; a force that is unmeasurable yet gives you a startling heroism to break through barriers. It originates from your heart, your soul and that passion that really matters to you. If you dedicate yourself to learn and spend the time discovering your truth, your own personal and emotional driving force, it'll set you free. By the end of this Elastic Attitude program and even joining our 7 week Coaching Program, you will develop a congruency Mind, Body and Soul.

It's time to take a look at and consider a few philosophies of mine to empower you to continue to shift your thinking. Remember, your thoughts become things. These ways of thinking will give you the strength to make new decisions and take the appropriate actions.

"NOTHING WORTH HAVING IS EASY TO GET."

When you really, really want something when do you want it? Yes of course, right here and right now. Though nothing worth having comes easy, it may well be simple yet it will require effort and that sweat equity. We have all heard the cliché:

"Rome wasn't built in a day."

So acquiring anything of value is going to take time, however, remember success loves speed. Other than in a children's well known fable, slow and steady does not win the race. I believe you will find that achievement is found through a journey of persistently and consistently striving towards your given deadlines and targets. It's this journey, the up and downs of life as you focus on growth, that cultivates your character. It's what builds new skills and you become worthy of what you desire and expect.

I ask you to spend a moment, think back and consider how you have stretched, even pushed through fear to acquire something of value to you. You see, to achieve anything of true value to you, you will have most certainly had to have stepped out of your comfort zone, more about this in a moment. You will have needed to focus on one course of action regardless of opposition or previous failure. You must persevere in order to succeed. As a coach, over the years I have seen so many people who have been able to perform and excel to the required standard to achieve all they believe desire and derserve. However the challenge for most people is staying on task, even having that emotional motivation in place. Yet even still, when someone has these pieces in place, the difference between someone achieving very little and that of the high performers is quite frankly

Chronic Inconsistency

So what is it that actually prevents you from doing what is necessary, remaining consistent and persevering? A common thing for many is the fear of failure; a commonly known acronym is:

False

Expectations

Appearing

Real

Everyone reacts in a different way, sometimes the fear of failure can either be motivating or paralysing. The fear of coming up short, not achieving all you said you would and the worry of looking like a fool for believing in your dreams. How would it actually feel if you aimed high and missed the grade? What actually would the consequences of your failure really be?

Imagine the feeling of the pursuit, the energy, the vibe you give yourself through getting involved and giving it your all. Remember, motion creates motivation. Personally I would rather be known as a dreamer, as someone that pursued happiness and someone that dreamed big dreams, rather than someone who lacked vision, never tried anything new and stayed confined by the shackles of negative thinking. What would you prefer?

Let me tell you my belief, although it's likely I haven't even met you; you are amazing. Every part of you is amazing; you were created in a certain way to be able to learn, develop and grow. I challenge you to embrace failure and to accept fear as part of your journey. Everyone worries a little too much; it's ok to worry, to be nervous, it shows that you care. I believe it gives you that edge. Worry is usually formed through feeling anxious of potential problems, yet in my experience, most people worry about things that never occur. Let's be honest, with all the worry of your past, you're ok right now hey. I'd like you to understand that the essence of life is built on ups and downs; the way the sun rises and sets, the ocean's tide comes in and out. Even the source of life for you; your heart expands and retracts. Ups and downs, life's rollercoaster some may say is evident in Mother Nature. Relax, stay calm and go with the flow of the ups and downs. What's essential here for your focus is to understand this;

If you focus on the depths of despair, worry, fear even failure, the ups and downs of life will take you there. However, if you focus on the elation, joy and the happiness success brings you, the ups and downs of life will take you there.

So remain calm, embrace fear and believe in your goals, be strong with your mindset to focus on achievement. What is the very worst that could happen? You give it your all and you miss the goal, yet you are further forward for trying. Motion creates motivation and the feeling, energy and excitement that comes from 'doing' is worth giving it your all regardless of the outcome. Fall in love with the process, give value without need of compensation and be proud of what you give. You will fail on your journey to succeed, that we know. Every failure is a lesson; it makes you stronger, builds character and is simply a rung on the ladder of progression. I would like to recommend a superb book, a short story entitled;

Go For No by Richard Fenton & Andrea Waltz

The message within the book's story is amazing and simply put, YES is the destination and NO is the journey. It will change the way you think about the word NO and the fear of failure. Grab a copy of both book and audio, listen, study and embrace the philosophies in your day to day life.

Something I have personally discovered over the years is that the flip side of fear is commitment; commitment to your goals, commitment to your family and to those that depend on you. A commitment to yourself and being the very best you can be. Success is a decision and at some point my friends, to get that endorphin fueled feeling of 'I DID IT', 'I AM A SUCCESS. You will need to go all in. Success needs your all.

I love surfing and back when I was travelling the world, the commitment to give it my all was occasionally fueled by the fear of making sure I didn't hit the rocks. It was the commitment and sheer effort that kept me alive. Shortly after this particular near death experience, I read this surfing philosophy from one of the great big wave riders of my time:

"Fear is a natural response, harnessing it is the tricky part. The key is not to fight it and not to analyse it.

*Trust yourself, trust your instincts and remember
the flip side of fear is commitment.*

*So get committed, lead from your heart, follow
your gut instinct and believe in yourself rather
than doubt and you will make it – that
I am sure".*

Another philosophy that has and continues to serve me well is to live on the edge. The edge of what you may well be thinking. The edge of your comfort zone. Stretching yourself at every opportunity. Earlier we touched on the fact that you have the ability to try new things, learn new skills and create new habits. The comfort zone that you live in is made up of the choices and decisions that are no longer a challenge to you; they are now easy. These things you will have once stretched yourself to do, like most new things at first, they are uncomfortable and to be successful you will need to be uncomfortable for a short period of time, it's how you grow. Interestingly most things of value to you, the things you crave and desire like:

FREEDOM

EXCITEMENT

CHANGE

WEALTH

HEALTH

SUCCESS

PASSION

BELIEF

LOVE

CONFIDENCE

DREAMS

These are often found where it is uncomfortable, outside of your comfort zone. I am confident that almost everything of value and importance to you, that you have acquired and achieved up until this day, you will have done so by stepping out of this self-imposed comfort zone. The goal, your desire, the need was stronger than the fear of being uncomfortable.

It was worth the risk, it was worth the challenge. It is quite breathtaking to see, when you are emotionally connected to what really matters, you'll act with a startling heroism.

To me this is what living is all about; that feeling of being on the edge, the excitement of doing something new, the fear of the unknown. This feeling you get when you have butterflies doing backflips inside your stomach, the feeling of being alive. Be prepared to keep challenging yourself, remember, development and growth is in YOUR DNA, live with the mantra 'One Life, One Chance.'

The final thing I would like to share with you in this chapter is the importance of the 'Power of Association'.

A mentor of mine Jim Rohn is well known for saying;

"Don't join an easy crowd; you won't grow. Go where the expectations and the demand to perform are high."

When interviewed about success and his personal thoughts on the main contributing factors, Tony Robbins suggested the number one contributing factor to be;

"The power of association."

Are you aware that your attitudes, your beliefs and even your bank balance are often a sum of the people you spend most of your time with? It is the power of association at work. Like the power of gravity, you are unable to see it, yet it's always working and is present around you every day. Have you ever noticed, when you spend a considerable amount of time with someone, you start to use the same terminology and vocabulary as they do, even picking up their accent? You will now, in fact you'll be aware of it already. When someone moves from a foreign country into another, they adopt the accent of the language depending upon where they live.

When I was in my early teens, on the occasions I was speaking with my family members from the Wirral on Merseyside, Liverpool, I would find myself mirroring and speaking with a scouse accent. They often thought I was mocking them, though aside from the odd "Alright our kid", it was actually the power of association at work. We all have this innate human reaction to mirror each other and fit in with our environment to feel comfortable and be liked. In this particular example, I believe it to be important that I was open to this influence. Because of my love and passion for all things Liverpool, including the accent, I was open to be influenced. I was fascinated and open to the association. I believe you are always being influenced in one of two ways:

"Unconsciously by association and consciously by inspiration."

From your early years, you have been programmed unconsciously through the components brought to you socially, environmentally and culturally so that you fit in. We are all chameleons in our own right, naturally adapting and evolving to fit the environment, be comfortable in our surroundings and ultimately to be liked. We have all been children. You may already have children of your own, either way you will understand the importance of having the right friends around you. You will know now, if you're a parent, even your parents with you, would have been conscious and aware of your friends. Are they of a good caliber? Are you in a safe and legal environment? No parent in their right mind would want their children spending time with local hooligans, smokers and drug abusers. Why? Because we are unconsciously 100% aware of the power of association.

Be conscious with 'who' you spend your time with. Choose to be around positive, happy, friendly, healthy, wealthy and successful people. I read a meme some time ago;

"You'll never fly with the eagles if you hang round with the turkeys."

This may sound harsh and it may be tough for you, however let's be straight. If you want to be successful in your field, if you wish to lead a better life than you lead today, then you will need to make tough decisions. These decisions will most likely lead to you changing and being more purposeful with 'who' you spend your time with. You must understand something here, I too have friends and family that I love and cherish. I respect them for who they are, their beliefs and what they wish for in their own life. Just because I choose a different path and because I choose to be associating with excellence in my field, does not for one minute mean I don't value time with these amazing friends and family. Even though I want to achieve my ambitions, I position myself purposely with those who are where I wish to be. Why? Because I understand the power of association.

If you wish to grow, if you want to unleash the passion that lies within you then you must first remove EVERY negative influence from your life and start today to be around people that:

- Share your ambition.
- That have already succeeded in your arena.

- Believe in you and your goals.
- Bring positivity to your environment.
- Are a radiator of good vibes and happiness.

Again it may well be a tough decision. Sometimes people are sharing a bed with negative, stinking thinkers. I highly recommend, if anyone brings anything less than the above to your life, spend little time with them, if any at all. Life should be full of an abundance of happiness and feeling loved, believed in and valued.

It's your environment through association that creates your beliefs, thoughts, actions and contribution. It's very important that you make the decision to now start making the power of association work for you, your goals and ambitions.

Start with finding mentors and inspirations, people that are really going to help you raise your game. Just by spending time with these people will naturally pull you up to the next level. Seek to be positively influenced by the best in your field. At the start there may be no one like this that you can directly associate with, though you must make it so. You can start with personal development, read uplifting books, listen to audio programs, attend events, invest in coaching programs and reach out to those succeeding in your field. Get involved!

If you want to be successful in your field, you have to do what successful people do and successful people influence themselves on purpose. Through the correct association, environment and personal development, these are key components to your success too.

Just to summarise this chapter on being elastic, shifting the way you think and stretching yourself to the next level. Here are a few practical points of focus:

- *Never question your ability, only ever question your activity. Get connected to your emotional driving force, it's this that will set you free.*

- *Be purposeful with who you spend your time, make sure YOU choose to put yourself in an uplifting environment where you are believed in.*

- *Respect yourself enough to employ yourself. Do something uncomfortable every day. Remember, everything worth having is at first uncomfortable to achieve.*

- *Plan to give more than is required each and every day. Go the extra mile, and develop a culture to stretch yourself and contribute without need of compensation*

CHAPTER 2- CREATING YOUR OWN DESTINY

'It is in your moments of decision that your destiny is shaped'

Have you ever wondered what it would actually feel like to be able to create your own destiny? To be 100% in control of your life, both now and in the future. Has it ever crossed your mind that life itself should be by your own design, rather than chance? It has become common in society, most people spend their life getting up and responding to what the day brings, rather than getting up living on purpose and with purpose to create the day ahead of them. Yes, it is easy to blame the environmental and social conditioning we have discussed, yet you have the power to choose, the ability to change and bring life, love and laughter to your day.

How is it that you currently shape your days? Are you living by design or are you living by chance?

It's amazing that when you shift the way you think, like we discussed in the previous chapter, you can change your whole concept of living well. By shifting the way in which you think and changing your beliefs to a thought process. that you are 100% responsible for your personal input and actions. Therefore you have the ability to design your own life and live on your terms. Yes, you are governed by rules and regulations, however you are still free to create a life of abundance. You may well still be thinking that it all depends on where you were born, what your childhood environment was like and what cultural and economic influences you may well of had? Though time and time again we are shown through successful stories of individuals throughout the world and in every arena, how individuals defeat the odds that are stacked up against them. We hear stories of desire, passion and a hunger to change and to succeed;

'It's your desire rather than ability that will determine your results'.

I had the pleasure of watching Olympic Gold Medalist Kriss Akabusi speak at an event a few years ago and something he said that day sticks with me and inspires me to avoid allowing excuses to hold people back. He said;

"The past is for reference, not residence."

I would like to share an event in my life that changed the way I thought and set me on the way to believe in the possibilities and start designing my own life. I had returned from travelling the world back in April 2001. During my travels I had lived the most amazing 16 months of freedom.

Looking back I was living on my terms. I was experiencing new cultures, discovering great adventures and living completely free. It was amazing seeing my family and friends when I returned, however the thought of being confined to the 9 to 5 working life of society scared the life out of me. It was then that I made the easy decision to work in the Network Marketing Industry. I could immediately see how having the freedom of being my own boss would allow me to still live on my terms. Back at this point in my life, being an entrepreneur was new to me and I still bared a mindset that you may be able to resonate with today;

"I incorrectly believed that wealth and financial freedom was for other people, those educated professionals, not someone like me."

Our beliefs literally dictate our lives and I believed that this goal setting lark was all mumbo jumbo, a load of hype that again was reserved for those that already had the trinkets of success. Maybe you can resonate with this crazy way of thinking. Maybe it has held you back too? What's fascinating to me now is that I had actually set a goal to save £10,000 with my ex-partner to travel the world, a goal we had achieved. Yet I still lived my life with this belief that goal setting is for those successful few. What rubbish. We all live our daily life by taking every action with an end goal in mind. Every step we take, every action is done so with a desired result. You are already a goal setting and goal achieving machine.

So back in 2001 at the young age of 23, I attended a business event, still holding on to that beach vibe in the way I appeared and to be honest I felt a little out of my comfort zone. I sat at the back of the room with 30 or so people in attendance. I was watching this gentleman in admiration. He was sharing his story about his successful life and how goal setting had led him and his wife to lead a life worth living. With all honesty I sat there a little closed to his words of wisdom, although I left that evening still feeling inspired and asking the question to myself "What if there is some truth around this goal setting idea?" My belief levels were low, but what if what he was saying, was true? What if I could earn a couple of thousand pound a month? That was huge for me. I was living back with my parents and that level of income would enable me to move out. I had the motivation and the desire. There was a goal there, a need. So I mentally set this as my target, even taking an A4 piece of paper and writing £2,000 income a month and sticking it on my wall as a reminder.

Over the following weeks my environment was changing, I was starting to engage with other entrepreneurs. What I now realise was, the Power of Association starting to work for me. I was attending more events. I was starting to discover that successful people lived the dream through personal development, goal setting and hard work. The power of association was shifting the way I thought. My beliefs and mindset about success was changing and changing fast. Then bang, out of the blue my best friend died in a freak motorbike accident. The really close group of friends left absolutely devastated to lose such an amazing young man. This was the toughest time of my life. Looking back now I believe that from every loss, eventually we gain strength. I realised back then that we don't have a crystal ball, and with my recent influence to start to goal set, I set about making the dreams my friend Jamie and I had together, a reality.

"From every adversity, comes a seed of equal of greater benefit."

I became passionate about living free, travelling the world and driving that black Porsche 911. I was going to do it for our friendship. It's bizarre I started to believe, I could see it and started to visualise my success every day and became a goal setting machine. Over the years I have studied the importance of goal setting, the power of the law of attraction and how we create our own destiny. There has been so much documented in the area of living an abundant life, the evidence and reference points of success are everywhere for us to see. My personal entrepreneurial journey has been rife with challenge, sleepless nights, massive personal growth, yet that emotional driving force just like in the 'Mountain People' story has empowered me to live the dreams I had while working for those I have. There is no secret. Through the rest of this chapter I am going to share with you the systems that will lead you to living a life of passion and goal achievement.

The challenge for you is to avoid lowering your expectations to match your environment. As discussed, changing your environment is fundamental to your success. You may not get all that you want, though you tend to get exactly what you expect. Start expecting success and expecting that desired outcome through the power of goal setting and goal achievement.

Let's start with your personal feeling about the word 'GOALS'. Everyone has an immediate response when they hear the word. Some people love goal setting, for others it can have a paralysing effect. I would like you to consider as we delve into establishing your truth, when I mention the word goal, if you need to change your response to a word that sits well with you then make that connection now. For example:

- Ambition
- Result
- Achievement
- Reward
- Accomplishment

Whatever works best for you is what is important here. To live in line with your emotional truth, to feel the power of living this way you have to discover what really matters to you. It is what will give you the strength and the confidence to design your own life with crystal clear clarity and certainty. What is now certain to you all is that you are driven by your emotions, from goal to achievement, from dream to accomplishment. You must spend time discovering that emotional connection; this internal drive will break through procrastination and fuel you to overcome any challenge with that pure passion to succeed. As we set out to work with you and establish this mindset along with specific areas of focus, I would like to ask you to ensure you carry out all tasks as we set them.

"To know and to avoid doing is to never really know."

So let's consider for a moment your personal core values in life. Our values are embedded in us from our initial upbringing and develop through the trials and triumphs of life. What would you consider to be your top 3 core values in life and why are they important to you? What values do you live your life by? For a moment please spend the time and write them down, please take the time to put a little depth into these.

1.

2.

3.

I would love to share mine with you too:

Love & Fulfilment - I will continue to wake up every day in love with being alive and a purpose to have fun in all I do. Personally I believe we must enjoy the process of each and every day, contributing to our environment and making a difference while living with our hearts on our sleeve.

Influence & Leadership - I read once, "Make a positive difference in someone else's life every day and yours will change for the better." We are all leaders and influencers in our own right. To be able to positively impact someone's character and behaviour for the better, is an extremely rewarding way to live your days. I personally will continue to be committed to be the wind beneath the wings of others, giving them the inspiration to be their best.

Loyalty & Relationships - The quality of life in my opinion, is determined by the quality of our relationships. It takes all of us for any one of us to succeed. Being committed to other's goals, beliefs and shared principles, is a great feeling. Time well spent, is time with friends and family.

If you have jumped this section, STOP. Go back and spend a few moments writing down your values and why they are important to you.

Remember I briefly shared with you my old thoughts, my old habits, that negative unconscious 'incorrect' thinking that success and goal achievement was reserved for other people. Well, let's consider the world in which you live in for a moment and let's shift you to see the truth.

With every sport, every game, every mission there is a goal, an objective a desired winning result. Every morning, as I have already touched on, you awake with an objective for the day, a goal, a must do for that moment, that day. Anthony Robbins calls it "Your current end picture." From the moment you wake, you have a human need to survive or to strive in the day ahead. Every action you take in life since the day you was born is done with this innate human need, goal setting. Goal achievement is in your make up. However, through the worlds conditioning of "I cannot", "You're not good enough", "That's for others", people have retracted to settling for 'their lot'. Why is it people spend more time getting excited about and planning a family holiday? Because conditioning states, that's all you can have. For many it's escaping from, rather than creating a life worth living. Why? It's the norm, people don't realise there is anything different or that they even have it within them, of which they do, and so do you!

Fundamentally goal setting is simply about getting excited, getting passionate about your life, realising it is ok to want more, to strive for more, to become more and achieve more. Like we discussed, what's holding people back is that fear, afraid of stretching, afraid of becoming uncomfortable and afraid of failure. May be this is the reason why so many people never excel, never try new things or even believe in the possibilities that lie within them, around them and before them. It's this mindset of mediocrity and an acceptance of under achievement that has become so common today. You are now already positioned from shifting your mindset and realising that it is in your DNA to learn, develop and grow. We now need to retrain your RAS, your reticular activating system to raise your game and start setting goals as you discover your inner passion. Trust me when I tell you, it is your birthright to succeed and live a life of abundance. So what is it you're passionate about?

Let's be straight, this is where the magic is, you will have heard on many occasions;

"When the why is big enough the how to is easy."

Yet most people are failing fast, have no drive and no passion to do the things they should be doing when they should be doing them. May be this is you and I will tell you why. Very few people, even you, truly develop a deeper motivation and connect with their own personal motivational truth. It is so easy to set goals in line with society and conditioning and this is what most people do. Now is the time for you to break free from this. It is important at this stage to get some solid beliefs in place and become resilient to outside influences, people that without realising are crushing the dreams of millions of people.

As you will already know, the entertainment industry is huge and massively influential in the world. As with everything you consume, it influences the way you think, how you act and even how you create your own expectations in life. It's easy to watch a life story in a 2 hour movie, and while often very inspiring and enjoyable, we unconsciously start to expect that same kind of immediate and instant gratification in our own life; but that is just unreal. Let me share with you the impact that 2 of the world's greatest movies can have on your unconscious mind and influence the way you think.

In the movie 'Forrest Gump', while speaking to a lady on the bench about his best friend Jenny, Forrest states;

"Life is like a box of chocolates, you never know what you're going to get."

How fascinating this statement is; one I believe strange and incorrect. At my ripe age of 40, every single box of chocolates I have ever opened, selected and eaten a chocolate from has had a little menu card inside it or even printed on the box. This menu card clearly and specifically tells you exactly which chocolate is which, so you can choose the appropriate chocolate in line with what you want and prefer. Can you see how a simple yet profound sentence, a sentence that is known all around the world can influence you into a life of mediocrity. According to a large number of ladies at a recent speaking engagement, they don't even need the menu card. They are already aware which chocolate is which and what they prefer. I believe life is exactly the same and I have personally discovered on my journey, that we choose. You are where you are today because of the choices and decisions you have made in the past. So it makes perfect and logical sense that you create your future with the choices, decisions and actions of today; you choose.

What will give you total confidence is that in almost every area of life you can seek appropriate guidance and direction in line with your taste buds, passions and ambitions. There is always a menu card, an instruction manual to guide you to get exactly what you want. So how I see this famous movie quote is different and true in real life;

"Life is like a box of chocolates, you can always choose and know what you're going to get."

In the movie 'The Pursuit of Happyness' Will Smith challenged his son saying;

"If you've got a dream, you've got to protect it. If people can't do something themselves they want to tell you, you can't do it. If you want something, you go get it, period."

I love this and how very true. Can you see how different words and phrases can impact you? Be aware of what you allow to influence you. Build that strength and resilience that only allows positivity into your internal environment. Remember this each and every day, no one has the right to steal your dreams, only you have the right to set them and go about creating them. It's time to break free and reclaim your dreams, goals and aspirations. I have often been asked "When is the best time to follow your dreams?" Well, the best time was last year; the second best time is right now. Ozzy Osbourne of the famous band Black Sabbath once said:

"Never let go of your dreams man, it's your dreams that make it happen."

It's time for you fall in love with the pursuit of your dreams, re-kindling and re-establishing your passion to succeed. Knowing that every day you're taking actions, and enjoying the process will give you a feeling of being alive. You have a chance to impact the world. What is the legacy you can create through turning your dreams into a reality? Consider the legacy and value the great. Walt Disney left the world through his personal vision and imagination. He was well known for saying;

"If you can dream it, you can do it! All of our dreams can come true if we just have the courage to pursue them."

Be courageous in the pursuit of your ambitions, even the most audacious ones. Remember, dreamers move mountains. Imagine for a moment that you could actually rub a magic lamp and you would be granted 10 wishes. As this is my book, I will play the genie and I have decided you deserve 10 wishes rather than 3. What would be your top 10 achievements, things and feelings that you would choose to bring into your life? What dreams and ambitions would you make come true?

1.

2.

3.

4.

5.

6.

7.

8.

9.

10.

It's really important when you start to set goals; you remove as much negative environmental conditioning as possible. Yes, many aspirations, goals and ambitions have and always will be triggered from society and other people's great achievements. This is ok, however you must spend time to discover your truth. What truly motivates you? It's the strength of your personal and emotional truth that will keep you going when the wind blows. You have to get out of your own head, so to speak and get congruent with what's in your heart; this is where your significant reason why is found. We will come back to this essential area of focus and discovery soon. For now let's dream a little more, let's get your creative energy flowing and open up the pathways of greatness.

You will I am sure over the years had so many goals and ambitions, things and achievements that come in all shapes and sizes. Imagine for a moment that anything was possible, what would you spend your time doing if health, time and money had no boundaries?

What would you achieve?
Where would you go?
Where would you live?
What would your life be like?
What would you experience?

What would you see?

Who would you share it with?

What would you do to make a difference?

There is only one star in your life. You are the leader, the creator, the influence and the goal achiever. Remember, it is in your DNA to be all these things and to learn, develop and grow. Imagine for a moment it was 10 years into the future and you are looking back on your successful life, a life of fun, adventure and contribution. Maybe like my night back in the Swallow hotel, yet this time it is you, the star of the evening sharing your stories of success. What would your perfect life look like?

Have you ever heard of a bucket list? It is a list of things you'd like to do in your life, before you kick the bucket. Start making your list right now. I have created a section here for you to get started and write a list of 101 things you'd like to do in your life. Ready, Steady, Go:

1.

2.

3.

4.

5.

6.

7.

8.

9.

10.

11.

12.

13.

14.

15.

16.

17.

18.

19.

20.

21.

22.

23.

24.

25.

26.

27.

28.

29.

30.

31.

32.

33.

34.

35.

36.

37.

38.

39.

40.

41.

42.

43.

44.

45.

46.

47.

48.

49.

50.

51.

52.

53.

54.

55.

56.

57.

58.

59.

60.

61.

62.

63.

64.

65.

66.

67.

68.

69.

70.

71.

72.

73.

74.

75.

76.

77.

78.

79.

80.

81.

82.

83.

84.

85.

86.

87.

88.

89.

90.

91.

92.

93.

94.

95.

96.

97.

98.

99.

100.

101.

So look, I guess like most people you may still have to complete your 101 things to do before you leave this amazing world, which is fantastic. So please make a promise to yourself and to me that you'll come back and complete that list of 101 things to do. Make that promise right now, that commitment to your goals, to your future and your personal achievement in life.

I would like to spend a little bit of time with you right now to take you to the next level of goal setting. What I'm going to do right now is spend some time on helping you discover that inner most passion; that significant reason why and that emotional driving force that enables you to break through procrastination to overcome any obstacle with startling heroism. Personally, I find this exercise really empowering and continue to spend time on myself, continually keeping focused on being in touch with my emotional motivation, my real truths and my significant reason why. How I do this is through the art of visualization, by spending time with myself considering what's really important to me and visualising my goals as a reality. After this exercise I'm going to piece together how you can really train your unconscious mind, that executive secretary to take you towards your goals instead of drifting further away.

Now this exercise is going to take 100% focus, it is a simple guided walk through to really unleash your creative energies and connect you to your personal truths. With this in mind I want you to understand that if you're reading the book you will need to go to the audio version and select this section, or go to this webpage now

http://www.elasticattitude.com/audioexercise

If you really are passionate about success, expanding your potential and reaching new heights then you must involve yourself with this audio walkthrough. If you are already listening to the audio, then that is fantastic.

I am confident, that through this exercise you will have had a feeling of empowerment, a rush of emotional energy and that feeling you get when the endorphins are flowing through your body and it makes the hairs on your arms stand up. To me, I liken it to the feeling of being like a kid in a sweet shop, or even my adult self in a Porsche garage. With this feeling I believe you will have discovered a true desire, something that has that important emotional connection to you. Be consciously aware of that feeling, consistently spending time putting yourself in the picture while you align your activities with making it a reality. Over the coming few days, take some time to go back and look at your bucket list and consider which of your goals sit well and align with your core values. This is a way to pull out what goals are really important to you through ensuring they sit well with your key values in life. Everything must be congruent, connected and in line for you as an individual. This is where so many people go wrong; consistently working for the wrong goals. You have the power now, through the knowledge you have learnt in this guided technique to put yourself in the picture of those goals you have extracted, get connected to the emotional power of each goal. Yes, it takes time, even a little solitude while you spend time with yourself, again valuable and time well spent.

In one of my all-time favourite songs 'Imagine' John Lennon sings:

"You may say I am a dreamer, but I'm not the only one."

This one line, from one amazing song has shaped my beliefs in the possibilities for others and for me. I believe in our dreams. Have confidence to be courageous in your dreams, you are not alone. You have a world of believers around you; sometimes you just have to find them. Through chapter one and chapter two we have focused on shifting the way you think, positioning yourself for success and unleashing the importance of what goals are really true to you. Remember, the outside creates the inside, and the inside is what shapes your thoughts, feelings and actions, this all in turn is what will create your destiny. So now I want to share with you how you bring these goals and ambitions to life in your conscious world first, so that you then train your executive secretary in your unconscious world, this is where the fun begins!

The first step we've already taken and that is the importance of writing your goals down. There is a science behind goal setting. Research shows that it is essential that you write your goals down because it actually triggers a different part of the brain and helps you take ownership of the goals from an unconscious perspective. Studies also show that you're 42% more likely to achieve your goals and dreams through simply applying them to paper. There are 3 different ways in which people learn, so taking this focus and mindset to the power of goal setting in my opinion, is really important.

The 3 ways of learning. Some people are auditory, some people are visual and some people are more kinesthetic. So we're going to activate the human mind. To ensure consciously and unconsciously, we train your executive secretary, your reticular activating system, to be conscious on creating pathways to achieve your goals and ambitions. You are going to do that in 3 ways:

1. Develop a descriptive list of the Goals, Desires and Ambitions you have activated in this chapter. Remember to put yourself in the picture when you write about them as if they are now, in the present, feeling and enjoying what they bring to your world.

2. Goal Boards. Creating a vision for your future. Over my years as a successful entrepreneur I have found goal boards to be really inspiring and empowering in helping me achieve my goals and ambitions. Still to this day I have my very first goal board I created back in 2001. It's amazing how sitting

down with the purpose of creating a board full of your goals dreams and aspirations can really be motivating and uplifting.

I would like to share a couple of stories with you that I find emotionally empowering that show how goal boards can really bring about the things you focus on. You may remember back in 2006 when the then worldwide phenomena 'The Secret' was published. I remember a story in The Secret about a gentleman that had moved into his dream house. He was sat in a room unpacking some boxes that had been in storage for many years. I believe his son walked over to him and asked what was in the boxes. He proceeded to explain to his young son what they were. When showing his son his goal board he started to cry, the house he had just moved into was the exact house he had pictured on his goal board. Not a similar house, it was the exact house. I remember watching The Secret DVD and the hairs on my arms standing up with excitement and pure amazement at the possibilities.

So this brings us back into my own personal story about goal boards and the power they truly do carry. Back in 2012 I decided to set five audacious goals that really resonated with me and to create five individual goal boards for each of my ambitions. The five goals I have are as follows:

A world sports tour in 2020 with my children, so they can watch passionate people excel at their loved profession. A 7 car garage to fulfil my childhood dream. To play the game of Monopoly for real, 4 green houses, 1 red hotel. A passion to contribute on a higher level with audios, books and coaching to empower the people of the world to believe in themselves and finally to live my Spanish dream.

I created 5 A3 goal boards that took pride of place in my office, and over the following 2 to 3 years I looked at them daily. Then when I moved through some changes in my personal circumstances, they went into storage. It wasn't until I was back in the UK for a weekend leadership event that I discovered my goal boards whilst I was looking for some other material. I was amazed to see how so much had been achieved and had already become a reality.

For example, the Spanish lifestyle goal board consisted of the ambition to be living in Spain with my children in a beautiful villa near the beach. I had pictures of a Jet Ski, a boat, and wakeboards. What's fascinating is, I have never really been great on boats., I must of just liked the picture at the time of developing the boards. What's fascinating is everything I had stuck to my Spanish lifestyle goal board had become a reality without me even realising. This is far from coincidence; it's the Law of Attraction, in action.

I challenge you to create your own goal boards today, and allow the law of attraction and the power of goal setting to work for you too. You will find you have so much fun putting this together. Pull all the family together and start to create an environment of goal setting and high expectation. I have been showing my little girls for a few years now. Every year we, well they, set goals in an Adventure book for the coming year and my mission is to help them tick them off. Along the way they write a journal of gratitude for all their adventures and amazing experiences. Start them young as they say; as a parent you have a responsibility.

3. Create your own mind movie. Creating your own mind movie is a unique way to take your own goals and ambitions and develop a 3 to 4 minute movie that you can watch at any time of the day. The idea here is to take your goals and aspirations, add them to show reel of existing successes and magical moments in your life. Choosing your favourite song and turning it into a 3 to 4 minute personalised movie. This is a phenomenal way to have gratitude and to be able to watch your own uplifting movie whenever you feel the need to be reminded of Your WHY. If you get over to the Passion to Succeed Facebook page you will be able to find a free video training on how to create your own mind movie. PM if you need direction. This really is worth doing.

Remember; a goal without a deadline is just a dream.

Now it leaves me to share with you the importance of savouring the journey and enjoying the process of chasing your dreams and bringing them to life. In today's society there can be an obsession with the destination; we do live in a results driven world. Just make sure you enjoy the process. Be grateful for all that you have, who you are, your vision, your passions and your ambitions. Though make sure you learn to savour the journey by;

"Giving value without need of compensation. Do it because you love it."

By working through this program you will be able to develop your own blueprint for success, a road map from A to B that has you focused on the daily activity while expecting only the best. Focus on your plan, your contribution and give your very best each and every day. Then, you will find the compound effect of a day well lived, will lead to your goals and importantly, what you give attention to from the tasks set out within this chapter.

CHAPTER 3- BEING ATTRACTIVE AND BECOMING THE GREATEST VERSION OF YOU

'Your greatness is revealed not by the lights that shine upon you, but by the light that shines within you'

We live in a world of attraction, everything is connected through the natural magnetism of 'like attracts like', yet we also hear how relationships flourish when couples are very much chalk and cheese. This creates an inner civil war in how we think and what we believe; a pull from one belief to the next. Every ethical and sincere individual brings a magic to this world, a personality and a vibe that attracts others. There is always someone you are attracted to in all areas of life somewhere in this world. We may share different values and personalities, yet more often than not, we are attracted to people like us and people who we aspire to be like.

Being attractive is far deeper than the skin It is so much more than being aesthetically pleasing to the eye. Every one of us carries a uniqueness, an energy and an aura that just vibrates and connects with others. Interestingly there is not one size that fits all. We are all attracted to different vibes, traits and feelings - different strokes for different folks.

Through my own personal experiences, I am 100% certain that attraction, for me anyway, comes from seeing someone happy, smiling and loving what they do. It shows in an energy, their posture, that sparkle in their eye. It's true:

"Beauty lies within the eye of the beholder."

So why is it that some people light up the room when they enter and others when they leave? My eldest daughter Isabella was sat with me in my office as she often does, creating and educating me in her wonderful ways as I worked. I was working on social media interaction on Facebook and she noticed a post asking What kind of person are you? A Radiator or a Drain. As inquisitive as a child is, with their childlike wonder for life, she asked me "Daddy, what does that mean?" I am sure you will have already come across the analogy, however I proceeded to explain to my daughter:

"People in the world have different ways of thinking, some people focus on the good and some on the bad. So a radiator is someone who brings warmth to their friends and environment, these people are warm, caring, passionate and considerate towards others; they are the radiators in life. Then we have some people that are always complaining about something. These people talk negatively about other people and their environment. They are the drains with their negative thinking sapping energy from those around them." Isabella quickly replied, "Well I am a radiator daddy." Of which I proudly replied "Yes you are princess!"

Over the years I have discovered that we are always influencing are own environment and we are 100% responsible for the energy we bring to our world and to those around us. What you say, does matter. How you make others feel, does matter. We have been conditioned to think the way we have, yet to keep allowing that to influence us as an adult or even young adult is a bullshit excuse to stay drowning in a sea of mediocrity and having a fear of change!! Successful people understand that we must expand our potential through consistently adapting our thinking. Always being solution orientated and seeking the opposite positive paradigm to any negative thought that could, for even a short space of time, allow you to become 'stinking thinking'.

When you look left and when you look right, you want to see uplifting influences, people that are also the wind beneath your wings as well as you being able to breathe positivity into their environment too.

So what influence is it that you bring to your world? Do you choose to be a radiator or a drain? This reminds me of something I have recently been sharing with my children;

"Small minds discuss people, great mind discuss opportunity, empowered minds discuss opportunity in people and for people."

I would like to challenge you to be someone who is known to have a love of bringing positivity and belief to and in others. It's attractive and it all starts with a genuine vibe towards people's well-being and success.

Why is it that some people just have this magnetism that draws people to them? It's an attraction that people just flock to be around them, to rub shoulders with them and even hang on every word. These people carry a 'charisma', a positive vibe, that of a radiator. You will probably already know, charisma is known to be the most attractive trait and one that is deemed to be something you either have or you don't. Why is it that some people have this charismatic ability to draw people towards them? Were they born this way? Are they attributes reserved only for a few? Well, let me be the bearer of great news, Charisma like EVERY other attractive trait, can be acquired through the power of modelling. Spend your time with radiators, spend your time with charismatic people and you will naturally develop this way of thinking that will shine from the inside out. I believe every one of you, have this magic in your DNA, an inner attraction just waiting for the right environment to set it free and truly expand your given potential. The question is, what stops you? What stops most people from allowing that inner beauty into the world? That personal magic of being YOU. Possibly lack of confidence, maybe through being in the wrong environment so far in your life? You see most people carry a fear of fitting in and being liked, when actually confidence isn't about will they like me, confidence is about I'll be just fine if they don't. For me personally, it goes back to a saying I am pretty confident that we all grew up being told this:

"If you have nothing nice to say then avoid say anything.""

Everyone has an opinion, yet what people think of you isn't your business, what you think of you, is. Believe in yourself, you integrity and your desire to contribute to this world. This program is about shifting the way you think, embracing change, embracing rejection and embracing that you have magic in your DNA. One thing for sure, change is inevitable, so now, today, is the day that you choose the direction in which you will change, learn new skills and embrace new challenges.

There are 4 simple philosophies that I wish to share with you in this chapter that should you focus on and follow, I believe you will be at the forefront of change. Consistently developing, growing and becoming more attractive in this ever-changing world we live in. They are:

1. **The power of words, tonality & vocabulary.**
2. **Creating first and lasting impressions in every encounter.**
3. **Developing better people skills.**
4. **Mentorship, modelling and association.**

These 4, possibly obvious points to you, are the building blocks of every great relationship and will position you to be more influential in all you do. What I will tell you now, is that like cultivating any new skill, these fundamentals will take dedication and effort to get right. You must as always be committed to developing new habits. These particular habits will help you become more attractive and draw people to you in less than 30 seconds. Remember, what I am sharing with you are my experiences that have and continue to enable me to live free and from my heart with a love and mission to positively influence the world.

1. The power of words, tonality & vocabulary

The words you use can really empower you to break free from the shackles of society, enabling you to live a more fulfilled life with deeper confidence and clarity in your future. The vocabulary we use is habitual and how we say things is so very important to our attraction and our relationships. We often here:

"It's not what you say it's how you say it."

So much communication nowadays is done socially through messenger, whatsapp, texts and so on, yet this way of communication sets everyone up for misinterpretation. It is very easy to read things in a different manner to what they are meant as there is no personality or tonality in a text. I will often train and coach entrepreneurs to understand texts are for information, your voice is for communication, remember this and it will serve you well. The vocabulary you use really does matter and the words of which you live by really can shape your environment too. What you say is what you see and what you see is what you believe; beliefs create feelings and in my experience, it is the inside that creates the outside. The terminology you use in your day to day life shapes, can even affect your attitude and your vibe that you bring to your arena each and every day.

I would like to run through an exercise with you to show you exactly what I mean, so you can see and feel it for yourself. This simple exercise is to show you exactly how this works, to get your mind thinking and to challenge you to change.

I am going to ask you a question, I will ask you this question 3 times and it is massively important that you understand this is where we need your verbal participation. What you will find fascinating, is that before each question I ask, I am going to give you the answer that I would like you to use. What is important here is that you answer the question out loud, so you may wish to get yourself somewhere appropriate. This particular participation is very important for you to 'feel' what I am sharing, it's how you will connect to this message. So if you're ready, let's get started.

The first answer I would like you to use, and remember to say it out loud is:

"I'M NOT TOO BAD."

So here is your question: "How are you today?"

Your answer: ***"I'M NOT TOO BAD."***

I wonder for a moment, how do you physically feel after answering a considerate question with an "I'm not too bad." Seriously, what is not too bad anyway? Who is responsible for starting this negative response and restricted vocabulary? Have you ever asked someone how they feel and wish you had never asked? These are the drains in life and it is this kind of thinking that leads to this response; it's the beginning of draining your own energy and that of others. Such a small sentence yet has profound impact and results. Just for a moment pay attention to how you feel with "I'm not too bad," your posture, your excitement and energy levels. I imagine your whole demeanour is of a low vibration; them endorphins are still fast asleep! You can see already how the words you use affect you on every level. Here's the thing, they are affecting others too.

So let's move on to the next response in our series of impactful answers. This time when I ask you the question, I would like you to answer again out loud:

"I'M OKAY."

So here is your question: "How are you today?"

Your answer: *"I'M OKAY."*

It's fascinating how words can make you feel. Again a simple and common answer around the world yet has a profound impact on your vibe. So how do you feel now? Slightly better maybe, still quite mediocre, just feeling ok right? No empowering feeling to put your heart and soul into the moment? The language you use has the power to re-shape your knowledge and expectations of the world you see. The words you use affect your attitude, so by changing the terminology and even your personal explanatory style, you are more likely to be happier and more optimistic.

I would like you to be more influential now, more optimistic with your answer. Let's make a difference in the impact your answer has on the way you feel. Let's raise that energy and vibration from the inside, ensuring you 'feel' the words YOU USE has on you, and your projection.

So what I would like you to do now is to use a word of your choice, albeit directed by me. This word must suit you best. I would like you to consider a word that's positive, something up lifting. Think of a word or phrase that has a truly invigorating response. Some of the responses I may use are:

"I'm sensational". "I'm awesome". "If I was any better I'd be triplets" and "I am fantastic thank you". This last one is my little girls' favourite. Pick something that suits you. Actually pick something that challenges you to speak in a more positive manner, even if it is abnormal to you;

"HOW WE CHANGE IS HOW WE SUCCEED."

SO YOU HAVE YOU THE ANSWER?

So here is your question: "How are you today?"

You must be able to 'feel' an immediate difference in how you feel, how you're holding yourself, your posture and even your facial expressions. The words we use are uplifting and do make a difference, if for some reason you are not getting this vibe then I would like to ask you to go back and start this section again...YOU MUST find your own empowering and uplifting response. If, however you have followed my instructions 100% then I would imagine you can feel the endorphins, the little 'happy people' I like to call them, bouncing around in your blood stream giving you a good feeling. How you feel is how you think and will directly enhance the energy you bring to the world, the choices you make and the actions you take.

Changing your terminology and that explanatory style mentioned already, will be a challenge in itself, just like the development of a new habit. It's almost like learning a new language, yet one you already know. The power of association, mentorship and modelling can be really influential here to and I will discuss later in this chapter. However, with your words and the resulting attitude, this can form you to position yourself to:

'Break free from the self-imposed shackles of mediocrity.

Go where expectations are high. Surround yourself with a network of positivity, high performance and the belief in each other's ability to shine'

Choosing this way, staying on task to learn this new habit of using positive words, will give you a more positive outlook and therefore raising that charisma in your DNA and attraction to others. By shining on the inside, your shine on the outside, it's your reflection. All of this is just the beginning of creating a positive environment, a bubble of positivity that will literally set you free. So let's take the next step, which I believe can be the toughest and possibly the biggest change required in your vocabulary.

We have briefly touched on the law of attraction, understanding like attracts like. What we put into the world we tend to attract back like a magnet of our thoughts, goals and ambitions.

"What we think about we bring about."

The human brain and the universal energy of the law of attraction has no knowledge or desire to separate your thoughts from positive or negative statements and requests. It will literally give you more of what you ask for and also more of what you suggest you don't want. So shifting the way in which you speak and focusing more on what you do want is going to work so much more in your favour. So the mission I wish to share with you here is to avoid using negative words and negative statements that consist of words such as:

Don't

Won't

Can't

Firstly you will become conscious of how often you use such negative words, then the challenge is to find replacement words. This will really stretch and grow your vocabulary enabling you to communicate in a far more positive and articulate manner. You literally need to discover a way to say things differently. I will admit it is difficult to and even very frustrating, yet persevere. This change will unconsciously have a massively positive impact on yourself and those around you. The environment you create starting with the centre and rippling out, will become one of high performance, positivity and an energy of everything is possible, if at first you just believe.

Let me share some examples of expressing yourself in a more positive manner:

Rather than say "Don't walk on the grass", you would say "Please walk on the path and avoid the grass."

Instead of saying "I can't speak Spanish," you would say "Sorry I am learning Spanish, do you speak English?" Lo siento, estoy aprendiendo Español? Tu habla Ingles?

Rather than say "I can't open this jar," you would say "Can you open this jar for me please?"

This may even seem trivial to you as you read, though every ingredient to becoming a more positive and greater version of yourself DOES MATTER. The concept of Elastic Attitude is about expanding your potential, developing new skills and going to the next level. I have found that this has personally raised my vocabulary and helped to make me the most positive person I know. Your brain has the capacity to continue to grow and open up new pathways to success. It's your mindset and beliefs that will help to shape your destiny.

So a positive answer to a simple question has the power to change how you feel. Using positive words, creating a positive frame of mind and winning attitude, changes your posture, raises your vibration and it shines through, naturally making you more attractive. Everything you learn and do on the back of this chapter is about creating good vibrations. The Beach Boys sang about this and what a great song, an absolute classic, fun and exciting song. Have a listen to it, search it on YouTube 'Good Vibrations by The Beach Boys'. It is such an uplifting song and I personally believe good vibrations are good for your soul. Remember, it's this positive mentality and the words you use that impacts your attitude. Your vibe is determined by your attitude in the moments of the day when no-one is watching. Having a positive outlook on life is your choice! You will have heard I am sure:

"It's your attitude rather than your aptitude that will determine your altitude"

How very true in the realms of success, happiness and being attractive. Having a positive outlook on life sounds easy and it is, however many people have been socially and environmentally conditioned to think in a negative way and use negative terminology. Yet I strongly believe if as an adult you continue to think this way when you have a choice, it's your fault. It is time to take back the control of your mind. You are the one who decides to have a positive outlook on life. There is always a silver lining to the clouds of doubt. You must create a new habit.

I was driving through a rainstorm recently and the way the sun lit up the sky behind the clouds was just breathtakingly beautiful. Right then on that day and in that moment, Mother Nature confirmed my beliefs; there is always sunshine behind the rain. What I mean here is, in every adversity, there is always opportunity. You just have to choose to see it by being solution orientated, by gaining clarity through contrast and having a paradigm shift from negative thinking to the polar positive opposite. This may be something unnatural to you, through past influences and ways of thinking, though right now my challenge to you is to seek the positive in EVERY situation and shape a new way of responding and creating.

Both of my little girls, Isabella & Alana over the last couple of years, have expressed to me their love of the rain as much as the sun, while we have been driving around the UK & Spain, simply because, you are unable to have a rainbow without both the sun and the rain. Just recently in fact my youngest little princess Alana, presented me with the most colourful and amazing picture of a rainbow, with a sun and some rain clouds again, showing me exactly this. I am truly blessed to have such positive and confident children, though I will, along with their mum take full responsibility for shaping an environment for them to think this way. Who is in your corner, leading you in the positive direction? Who is mentoring and coaching you to think in a way that will enable you to live a fruitful and positive life?

A well known mentor of mine Jim Rohn is famous for saying:

"The same wind blows on us all. It's how you choose the set of your sail that will determine your outcome and destination."

You are 100% in control now. You are aware of how you can and must think in order to live a healthy and successful life. From every adversity comes a seed of equal or greater opportunity...choose to seek it and feel it, in how you show up in your daily life.

2. Creating first and lasting impressions in every encounter

Are you aware that you have between 7 & 17 seconds to make that all important first impression? This can be quite daunting for even the most confident of individuals, yet the key is to be true to you as with everything I am sharing with you. Being yourself at core, is essential to feel good.

You are amazing and unique. Every single human being has a place in this world along with the inner strength to decide at any time to be strong and confident. When fear presents itself, you must command and demand in your mind the power to take control of your state, your thinking and your beliefs. You have the power to say "YES." You can overcome any obstacle that presents itself to you and then give it your all, being unequivocally you. Now have the confidence that you bring something special to every encounter - YOU.

First impressions will either open or close doors for you. What's interesting and something to be conscious of is, you never know when, where and at what time in your life that the importance of making a good first impression will be so important to you. I am pretty confident in your life already you have had moments when you wish you had presented yourself in a different way, said something less embarrassing and shown more interest in someone else. Understand this is ok, it's human nature to make mistakes, though to keep making them, to never learn from them and to avoid making the required change, is crazy.

In this section I would like to share with you how you can make that fantastic lasting and leaving impression. I am going to share some simple areas of focus and techniques. Remember, you're the product, always be prepared to sell yourself as the greatest version of you.

We have talked about positivity, your posture, your vibe and being more attractive. It is all to do with feeling good and confident, so dress for success too. How we look and take care of ourselves is again essential to how we feel. Grooming in today's society is almost expected. We all make an effort at times to look great, smell great and feel great, we have a desire to fit in to our environment and be liked. You will already know the beauty and fashion industries are 2 of the biggest and most competitive in the world today. The thought process and importance behind dressing for success, is 'knowing' you never have a second chance, to make that first impression. It's too late to think "I wish I'd had a shave this morning," "I wish I had done my make-up," "If only I had made more of an effort."

I am sure you will have heard in conversation at some point in your life; "When in Rome do as the Romans do". This simple statement is a philosophy about acting appropriate to the environment you find yourself in; being respectful of laws, languages, cultures and traditions in other countries and other people's homes. I am a lover of travelling, I love getting involved, seeing other ways of living, cultures and always being respectful to where I am, even modelling myself to fit in and conform to local rules.

Back in 2001 I spent the most amazing weekend in Rome, I had recently returned from travelling the world and started my entrepreneurial journey in the Network Marketing Industry and this weekend away was a reward for my achievements in the first few months. I was spending the weekend with super successful people, people that inspired me and that I aspired to be like. We were staying at the Cavaleri Hotel which sits on one of the twelve hills overlooking the beautiful city of Rome. This hotel was exquisite, actually it was my first ever experience of staying in a 5 star hotel and still to this day after 17 years of travelling the world 5 star, it is still one of the most amazing and opulent hotels I have ever stayed in. Interestingly prior to going away, I realised if I wanted to succeed in this entrepreneurial high performance environment, I was going to need to dress for success. I needed a suit for the conference and a dinner suit for the black tie gala dinner. Who was going to take me seriously if I didn't make an effort to dress appropriately, turning up as the surfer dude I had been whilst travelling?

I would like to share a brief yet impactful story with you and I challenge you to set a goal; go to Rome one day and maybe you will observe exactly what I did. We all know the reputation the Italians have for fashion and setting trends on the catwalks of the world; it's this passion to dress for success that I'd like to share.

That weekend I had the most amazing time with fellow high performing entrepreneurs, business partners and multi-millionaires. These people have become great friends through the magical experiences we had with all that Rome had to offer; from giant barrel barefoot grape crushing competitions, to being escorted from the Colosseum by security for re-enacting the Gladiator movie. Yet it was my walk to a local shop that left a lasting impression, an impression that changed the way I think, making me always conscious to dress for success on every occasion.

It was the final day of this fantastic trip following a fun fuelled gala dinner that carried on into the early hours of the Sunday morning. I smoked back then, and feeling a little delicate from the red wine the night before, I decided to walk down to the local shop to buy some cigarettes. It was around 9 am and quite honestly I hadn't made much of an effort in my appearance, you could say I looked a bit of a mess. What was evident as I strolled the streets was that the locals looked and dressed sensational for a simple walk to the local shop for the Sunday paper. I observed how everyone walked with confidence, there was a strength in their presence and a power in their voice as they spoke to one another in the shop. At this point I was personally the complete opposite. I was feeling a little embarrassed with how I had presented myself, it clearly impacted the way I felt. I was almost arched over, lacking confidence simply because I hadn't made an effort with my appearance and it showed. I wonder what they thought about me; I am guessing it was in huge contrast to how I looked at them. Actually, I bet none of them remember at all, yet I remember the detail, the greetings and the energy and positivity they all gave off. Who left the lasting impression on that day?

How you feel is so important and dressing for success is paramount. Now when I say dressing for success, let me explain. I am suggesting that you dress to feel great; you dress appropriately for the environment you're entering. I am 100% confident at some point you have left your home and felt a little uncomfortable with what you were wearing. You became aware that it was making you feel a little self-conscious. It's crazy; it could even be as simple as your belt that is making you uncomfortable, maybe you have the wrong shoes on, the blouse you're wearing doesn't feel great, maybe you're even wearing Tuesday socks on a Monday! Every one of you has felt this way at some point, maybe too often, yet you carry on with your day as you're in a rush and it seems insignificant. You then spend all day feeling uncomfortable, although to others you probably look fantastic in the way you dress. However this 'uncomfort' affects your posture, your confidence and your vibe. Can you see why dressing for success, feeling great with what you're wearing and how you look will impact your forthcoming first impressions. Next time this happens, because it will happen again, turn around go back in your house, make the change required and leave your home into your environment feeling great. It will impact your day positively, giving you strength and confidence in all you do.

The biggest result in this awareness and appropriate action is the feeling it gives you. Your biggest accessory in life is your smile. Personally I love to see someone smile, everyone around the world adds a beauty and an energy to the world when they smile; it's contagious. A smile is the most attractive element of being you. A smile when you greet people is always mirrored back to you. It's a natural response to smile back at someone who smiles at you. Here's an interesting thought, are you aware that if you're feeling a little negative, frustrated even, maybe annoyed at an outcome; smile, it naturally removes negative vibes. You are unable to be angry, negative and annoyed when you smile, so smiling with every new encounter opens people up to that attractive first impression you give.

All of this sets you up to make that lasting impression because you feel great, you have an air of confidence and give off this positive energy; your charisma proceeds you. Once you have position, your internal strength and confidence, everything I believe, now rests with the importance of a great greeting, a firm, confident and considerate hand shake, a smile and showing a genuine interest in the person you are meeting, even greeting. My advice is this, smile with confidence, mirror the handshake style of your counterpart and speak with an energy and interest in your question:

"How are you today?"

Remember your own response to this magical question.

3. Developing better people skills

From an early age we aspire to be like others, we naturally and unconsciously mirror others with a purpose to fit in, be like them and feel comfortable within our environment. Good people skills and a kindness towards others is at the centre of living a life of fun, rewarding and loving relationships. You can read, study and learn so much on the subject of people skills, communication both verbal and non-verbal in a short space of time, however it will take a lifetime to master. I personally believe, if you respect each other's beliefs and you chose to be considerate to others well-being, happiness and their success, then good people skills come naturally. My mum, a lady that has spent her life coaching and mentoring thousands of entrepreneurs in the direct selling and network marketing industry is famous for saying:

"Rely on no-one yet VALUE EVERYONE"

What a fabulous way to look at the world we live in. Valuing everyone for what they bring to your relationship, however big or small that contribution may be. It may sometimes be different to how you would be and act, though it's important here to remember that it's ok and other people's beliefs are as important as yours. It's your response to an event, to others communication and contribution that will create your desired outcome; remember we chose our personal decisions and actions. So yes rely on no-one, yet truly value everyone.

I have a fascination and love for people. From an early I have always loved to listen, watch and learn from others, often finding myself engaged in the moment so much that the rest of the world disappears so to speak. Communication is at the heart of every great relationship, how can you build lasting and fruitful relationships without spending time listening and speaking with others? Writing and creating this program for me feels great because I am ticking my desire to contribute and positively influence others. However it can be quite soul destroying being separated from speaking and communicating with others. I find that a few hours at a time is enough for me before I have a need to engage with others; it's in our DNA to associate and be around people. Consciously ensure you spend some of your time each day to learn about friend's experiences, ask and listen to their dreams and passions. When you do this you will discover that it can be both fascinating and inspiring listening to people's challenges, adventures and how they persevered to succeed.

"The quality of our life lies within the quality of our relationships."

In Steve Shapiro's book 'Listening for Success' he talks about, "If you're there, be there." In today's social lifestyle everyone is always on their phone, it's a challenge to stay in the moment with those you are actually present with. As an entrepreneur I too like you I imagine, find myself easily distracted by all communications hitting my phone You must all be conscious and when you are there, be there in that moment, get lost in the moment when connecting and conversing with others. Showing up is no longer enough, be present and show people you are emotionally available to connect and to build new relationships.

It's just great to meet someone new, build a new relationship, even rekindle an existing friendship you have. Remember, always be open, be warm, positive and respectful to other people's beliefs. As we have already touched on, we all have different beliefs. Good people skills is having an awareness to other people's feelings and respecting their beliefs even if they differ from yours. Always remember this because you know how strong your own beliefs and feelings to you are too. Everyone has great strengths; you all have something to contribute, positively influencing others and spreading good feelings. The little things in life throughout the day really do matter. Consider for a moment, how often in life do people feel valued and appreciated? Frustratingly it has become so uncommon. Be grateful, complimentary and show gratitude; go out of your way to hold the door open for someone, let someone know they gave you a great service, tell someone they look great, thank someone for what they have done. An act of compassion is good for the heart and it feels great too. Develop an empowered mind to positively influence others; small minds discuss people, great minds discuss opportunity, empowered minds discuss opportunity in and for others. Your mission, in my opinion is to leave every encounter better than you found it; be the wind beneath the wings and remember the cliché:

"If you have nothing nice to say, then avoid saying anything."

As a driven individual you will always be in an environment and position to develop new relationships both personally and in business. You may need to be the one to step out of your comfort zone and initiate conversation, by greeting people with that positive vibe, smile and hand shake we discussed earlier. New opportunities to develop new friendships will always present themselves; ask questions show a genuine interest and look people in the eye when you talk with them. Listen to what others have to say, learn to be present and avoid doing what most people do when they're waiting for their turn to speak; just thinking of what to say next. When you take a genuine interest in others the conversation will naturally flow with ease.

Some key things to remember when developing new relationships are:

1. The number one word people love to here and always here in a crowded room is their own name. So when you are speaking with people always use their name in conversations. For those of you who believe you never remember names, it's simply because you avoid using them. Use them, you'll remember and people will warm to you.

2. What is it most people love to talk about? Yes, themselves. So by showing a genuine interest in others, asking open questions, using their name and discussing their experiences and life, they will gravitate to you, building an instant rapport.

3. Mirroring is the key to duplicating human excellence, it's how we learn, develop and grow. It is also possibly the most important art of communication and building strong and lasting relationships. Let me explain. We subconsciously and instinctively switch our body position and posture to match that of another person we are communicating with, we all do it and we have been doing from birth; even prior to being born, when you mirror the rhythm of your heart beat with your mothers. Mirroring non-verbal communication is a way of building an immediate bond and the

foundation to connecting with others. When done with the right intent and subtly allowing your body to mirror the movements and body positions of others, it is scientifically proven to gain warmth, rapport and an openness to communicate freely. So try this, it starts with observing a person's body positions, if they have their arms crossed, then slowly cross yours. If they lean back in a chair, then subtly lean back too. I have tried this in many business engagements and I have consciously been quite extreme with my actions and mirroring, removing the subtle actions and being quite obvious, no-one has ever consciously noticed what I am doing. Try it for yourself.

You can also mirror terminology and tonality in the same manner, which has the same impact as mirroring body language. You are simply talking with someone in the way in which they like to communicate, which means they will naturally warm to you and also understand you. I often talk with colleagues and those I coach with the importance of being the chameleon so that it enables us to converse and get the very best out of them. Mirroring your surroundings to fit in, yet stand out, builds relationships fast and effectively.

This rolls into my final strategy for you to unleash that attractive charisma you have within your DNA, quite perfectly.

4. Mentorship, modelling and association

Earlier I shared with you the importance of the power of association, how we become a sum of the people we spend most of our time with. Positioning yourself in the correct and empowering environment along with selecting the best mentorship is essential for you. Why you may ask? Mirroring as you now know is something you do instinctively, so by modelling success through mirroring successful people, will raise your opportunities, this is why now you must now chose to associate with the right people. You must now work hard to position yourself to be influenced by the best in your field, seek out a mentor, find a coach and get yourself on a personal development plan so that you feed your mind with success principles and develop an unstoppable mindset. This is what will set you free and give you the strength to break through your self-imposed glass ceiling. Your personal mission is to always be open to a positive and success based influence.

In the about the author section I shared with you how having two great parents really was an amazing foundation for me for which I am forever grateful. What you may yet to be made aware of, is that my mum Jackie White, has also been a huge influence in the Network Marketing Industry throughout Europe. She, over the years, has become the benchmark for success, I may well be a little bias here, however it is true. I hope she completes her book soon, so that you can all share in the influence thousands of us have had. For now I would like to share a story she once told me, a story that will one day surely appear in her book.

Back in her early twenties, at the beginning of her career, she was very shy, although aspired to be like this extremely successful lady, a lady who to my mum was an image of success. She made a decision to purposefully copy, mirror and model herself on this successful woman. She started to dress for success just like this successful woman, and mimic all the stuff that we instinctively do to fit into our environment. It amazed me listening to this story. I had never known my mum to be shy or lacking confidence since the day I was born. It fascinated me how my mum went to the extreme, changing her vocabulary, changing the way she walked and even starting to smoke so to exactly mirror this inspiring woman. This mindset and ambition to focus on the modelling of a mentor was all in line with a desire to succeed and walk the path of success. Over time, my mum duplicated everything this lady did becoming alike her in so many ways;

it really helped her gain confidence, self-belief and a certainty in her own success. This natural human behaviour is what I am suggesting you do now. It is time for you to model success rather than accept mediocrity. Top selling author and leadership expert Jack Canfield often talks about:

"Act as if and then you will become."

I personally believe in every arena, in any path you may choose, you have been inspired by successful people and then aspire to be like them and succeed like them in that given field. Just like when Roger Bannister first ran the four minute mile, he set a standard and opened up the doors for others to believe it was possible. Find successful people in your field, find out what makes them tick, what is it they have done and continue to do? Your own mission is to make your personal plan like we discussed earlier, with character traits, to learn the reference points of their success. Have the confidence to get in touch with them, may be even offer to take them out for dinner. Ask them, as one of the best in their field, an expert in their arena, would they be willing to share some time with you to pick their brains, so you can learn from them. If they have coaching and mentorship programs, get involved, make the investment of money and time to become the greatest version of you.

You are going to be influenced by your environment; you will naturally mirror and model yourself on those around you anyway. Have the awareness to choose on purpose and choose wisely. Remember, we become what we consume.

So what's next for you, what are your personal key areas of focus to become more attractive in all you do? I would like you to take the time now, no jumping to the next section. It's time to develop your own areas of personal growth. In the below section write down at least 5 points and make a plan to establish the new skills required.

1.

2.

3.

4.

5.

CHAPTER 4- THE BALANCE OF TIME

'If you love life, avoid wasting time, for time is what life is made up of'

When you really, really want something, when do you want it? Yes, of course, right now. When you learn to take this urgency into your daily tasks, with a passion to get things done despite any obstacle or self-imposed procrastination, then your opportunities will really start to soar.

Remember we discussed in Chapter 1: Success Loves Speed. Slow and steady never wins the race, however persistent and constant urgency does. Using your time with purpose and urgency is what enables you to thrive and can help to stop you wasting the moments of today that so many people do. You are all aware of how time can seem to fly by so quickly; how children grow up so fast and how its April already when Christmas seems only days ago. Personally I have learned how to savour the journey and enjoy the moments of today. Let's be straight, the only time that truly matters is right now, this moment, being present and aware. There is always something amazing happening in every moment of the day. I would like you to become tuned in to being aware and being present, living each moment to the best of your ability and enjoying the process.

The challenge is, time is what people crave the most, yet it is typically what people use with least respect and dedication, allowing time to drift by. The objective of this chapter is again to shift the way you think and importantly how you use your time, so that you can learn to prioritise and stay on task. The hurdle you have is, we live in a quick fix world, a microwave society of expecting immediate results. The human race has become experts at finding and developing solutions, in order to make life easier. However, what the general public never sees is the time it has taken to discover and develop these solutions. Very much like success, so often success is seen in the celebration of an achievement, reaching a milestone, winning a race and being awarded an accolade. However, success is won in the moments of decision when no one else is watching. High achievement is acquired through hours upon hours of dedication on the mission in hand. It's found with a consistent focus to develop skills, burn the midnight oil and overcome every challenge on the road to success in EVERY arena. It's in these moments when success is won. Things do naturally take time and effort to cultivate into a reality. As we discussed previously, it's the social and environmental conditioning of the past that has shaped the way we think and these expectations we have. The TV has become such a huge part of everyone's life; it's almost a way for people to escape from living and living well. A friend of mine once told me;

"People on the television make money, people who watch it don't."

Remember, everything is influencing you at all times, both consciously and unconsciously. What you generally see on the television as a whole sucks you into thinking that way, expecting those instant results we discussed, that are often portrayed in a movie or on particular programmes. Yes, I watch TV too, however I tend to watch things that are inspirational and uplifting. Specific movies maybe, or watching people compete passionately in their preferred sport, or watching things with my children where other children are aspiring to be their best they can be, like Britain's Got Talent or similar. How you chose to spend your time is ultimately how you will live your life. Time is clearly our most precious asset, it is essential you use it wisely and in line with your goals and ambitions.

We have spent some time and focused effort over the previous 3 chapters establishing a way of thinking, discovering and connecting to your emotional truth. It is now your top priority to marry up the level of contribution required to feel fulfilled in all you do. A great book I read many years ago really shifted my thinking and understanding of time contribution, it was called 'Dare To Dream and Work To Win' by Dr. Tom Barrett. He shared a simple story about airline pilots. Was you aware that when airlines interview pilots for a new position, one of the main interests as an employer is 'Flight Time'. Interestingly the length of time someone has been a pilot is far less important than the hours a pilot has spent flying in the sky; 'Flight Time'. You could be in business, sport, learning a new language, even in a relationship for years, expecting results and happiness, however over the years what time have you actually contributed to cultivate this area of your life? What has been and what is your 'Flight Time'? Be aware and consider your Flight Time from now on.

It is very easy to carry on in the same way of thinking and everyone does it, everyone wants and expects immediate results. I am guessing that most of you at some time in your life have had a desire to gain weight, lose weight, get fit, develop muscle and even discover that hidden 6 pack. You may have been on this journey too; you change your diet, start going to the gym and everyday look in the mirror and jumping on the scales looking for results. However, deep down you know things worth having take time, focus and dedication to cultivate into a reality, yet you still look for immediate results on a daily basis. This is habitual behaviour and in this chapter we are going to change the way you think and develop new habits to enforce your contribution. Ultimately what will give you a level of success is your personal contribution of time to anything and everything, it could be a relationship, a sport, business or even education. Before we leap forwards, it is important that you know and also understand the importance of the foundations we have set in the first 3 chapters:

1. **The way you think is what will shape your destiny.**
2. **Having that emotional driving force is what empowers you into consistent activity.**
3. **How you show up and be the greatest version of yourself brings value to the moments of today.**

It's these 3 foundational chapters that will set you free to focus on your time contribution, enjoying the process and allowing true momentum to develop. As momentum develops the compound effect will take place in all areas of life. It's these 3 chapters that will give you the mindset to allow and push this to happen. Diligence is key so that the compound of you taking the right actions at the right time take place, and over time give you the results your effort deserves. Always consider your flight time. I have discovered over the years and live by this philosophy of mine;

"Never question your ability, only ever question your activity."

You will have all heard many sayings over the years, such as:

- *Nothing worth having was easy to achieve.*
- *There are no shortcuts to anywhere worth going.*
- *Rome wasn't built in a day.*
- *There is no such thing as get rich quick.*

Understanding these philosophies while having an element of patience is essential as you develop your business, empire and legacy. You already know in your heart, if you want to build it right, it will take time, energy and sweat equity. Your life is no dress rehearsal, you all have your time on this earth to make a difference and influence your world. What will you be remembered by? What would you do with your time, if you were certain of the outcome? If you had complete certainty what would you be willing to give? Many years ago a mentor of mine asked me a question, he said;

"Craig, what would you do if your success was guaranteed, if you was 100% certain of the outcome and all your dreams and aspirations became a reality. How hard would you work? How much time would you give to achieve your desired result? Would you do whatever it takes? Would you burn the midnight oil? Would you study and follow the success path of others 100%?"

I ask you, what would you be willing to give, to learn and to sacrifice? This simple question had a profound effect on me because I saw in the question, if I focused on my contribution and the time I was willing to give, through action and effort I'd be guaranteeing the results myself. Certainty is certainly a powerful force in carving out a successful future. You will be pleased to know that self-made millionaires share common traits and habits that you can create and live by too. They are goal setters, they decide on their desired outcome, they develop a strategy. They create a plan of action and then commit to working their plan every day until successful. You too can develop this kind of focus and road map to succeed; it is then about consistently stretching yourself to succeed and making a decision to push:

Persevere

Until

Success

Happens

We discussed the in the first chapter the importance of pushing to the end, and pushing until the finish line.. I believe it is human nature; you are driven emotionally to work with deadlines, to get things done. Think for a moment, you book a family holiday 10 months in advance. Over the coming 10 months you have a list of things that need doing, prior to taking off around the world on your dream holiday. When would you say that you would typically get these things done? Yes, like most people in the last week, even the last day as you have a 'do or die' deadline; it has to be done or you miss going on holiday.

In business I like to familiarise this natural innate human trait to that of a marathon runner, it's a way to focus and to get ahead while then striving for growth. A marathon runner will typically have their own game plan, a plan that meets their ambitions to be their best, achieve their goals and even win the race. The plan will often be to get off to a fast start, putting that energy and focus in the take-off from the line and getting ahead of the pack so that they can lead the way, running their race without any 'argy bargy', elbows and feet clashing so to speak. Then once they have set the pace and got ahead they look to settle into a strong pace, a pace that stretches them yet a pace that they can consistently perform to, for a long period of time. Then like every human being, when the end is near, the finish line is in sight, when we are starting to feel sapped of energy, they have this rush of endorphins finding that extra energy, that extra gear and they accelerate, pushing themselves right over the line to achieve their best.

This philosophy is one that if you position yourself to work to short deadlines, 4 weekly, monthly, quarterly, daily even, you can learn to push yourself beyond your own expectations and achieve new heights. I run 4 weekly leadership events; this is a great opportunity for entrepreneurs to engage in this philosophy, driving their businesses from event to event. Look around you, what events can you engage with on a regular basis, to give you deadlines to run from and strive between. Find an event, get committed and push yourself. On my 7 week coaching program, you get access to a 5 weekly lifetime mentorships webinar, this could be an ideal platform for you to become and be your very best. Feel free to contact me today and get involved.

So I'm just curious, what is your personal philosophy to time? How well do you use it and how do you value your time and the time of others? Time is well known and documented to be our most precious asset, something we should use wisely as life is no dress rehearsal right? I am sure you will agree, as you grow older, learn new skills and have your own family, you start to appreciate time, even look at it differently, with time. If you have children, I believe this really highlights how time can fly by, how you can miss the magic when you allow it to drift by. I have 2 amazing little girls, they are growing up fast. Watching them grow and continually develop gives me an appreciation of the quality time I have with them, making the most of every step of their life. When you are there, be there. Many years ago my mum shared some interesting words with me called the Bank Account of Life. I believe it opened me up to a different way of thinking and how I appreciated time. I hope sharing this with you today also makes you realise just how precious time can be.

"The Bank Account of Life."

Imagine there is such a bank that credits your account each morning with £86,400. It carries over no balance from day to day. Every evening it deletes whatever part of the balance you failed to use during the day. What would you do? I am expecting you would draw out every penny and use it wisely? Surely you would learn how to use, spend and invest your money well? Well, each of us has such a bank, its name is Time.

Every morning it credits us with 86,400 seconds. Every night it writes off as lost what you have failed to use in good purpose. It carries over no balance; it allows no credit and no overdraft. Each day without fail it opens a new account for you, and each night it burns the remains of the day.

Time is constant; the seconds of your life are always passing by. You must learn to value time and invest it wisely and in line with your emotional motivation to be your best. As far as I am aware you are only here once, be conscious of living well. The question I have for you is, how will you be remembered in years to come? One thing is for sure, it's the dash of time that counts. Apologies for the sombre vibe, however every one of us passes at some point. We are often remembered in cemeteries as a doting parent, loving partners and great friends. On every engraved tombstone I have seen it always shows the year someone was born and the year they passed. What's important is the dash between the years, how you used your time, made a difference and contributed to positively influence your world. It's the dash that counts, how will you be remembered for using your life to the full?

My challenge for you is to break free from the mindset and constraints of society, a society that is about conformity rather than individuality. Generally everyone has been brainwashed to go to work for 8 hours a day, sleep for 8 hours a day and typically waste 8 hours a day, commonly known as Groundhog Day. This mindset of getting a job for life, settling for your lot and following the crowd only leads to a life of mediocrity and for most feeling unfulfilled.

I believe and have 100% confidence we are at the beginning of worldwide change, change that will see huge growth in the entrepreneurial age, huge growth in people working at something they are truly passionate about either as an entrepreneur or in a job role. An age where people are hungry for personal growth, fulfilment and a feeling of really living well and making a difference. You must be the one that right now chooses to break free from the chains of mediocrity. Make a decision to retrain your mind, retrain your body clock so you can make the grade and live on your terms. Every moment, every second counts, consider these points for a moment:

To realise the value of one year, ask a student who failed the grade.

To realise the value of one month, ask a mother who gave birth to a premature baby.

To realise the value of one week, ask the editor of a weekly newspaper, magazine or blog.

To realise the value of one hour, ask the lovers waiting to meet.

To realise the value of one minute, ask the person who just missed the train.

To realise the value of one-second, ask the person who just avoided an accident.

To realise the value of one millisecond, ask the person who just won Silver at the Olympics.

I am sure you can see and will already agree, time is our most precious asset, once it has gone, that moment is gone forever. Throughout the rest of this chapter I would like to share with you how I have managed to learn to use my time wisely, being on purpose and using the time each day in line with my emotional motivations and core values in life. Again

I must stress the importance of the first 3 chapters, everything is connected and a piece of your life's jigsaw.

"Life is not about the breaths we take; it is about the moments that take our breath away."

Every one of you deserves this feeling on a daily basis. When you're aware and in the moment, there is always something happening, always something amazing to see. Would you agree you are where you are today because of the choices, decisions and actions of the past? Of course. How you have used your time has led you here today; how you have lived is what has given you these breathtaking moments and even an abundance of challenge too. Remember, how we change is how we succeed and having an appreciation for the challenges makes the magic even more rewarding. So now is the only moment that truly counts. Your decision in this moment to live in the now, profit from the past and plan for the future is the beginning of change, and using your time better. The moments of decision when no one else is watching can be your personal trigger and this is the first thought process that I would like to share with you.

This simple process is the start of developing a new pathway, a new habit to do the right thing at the right time, for you. Ask yourself on a regular basis:

"Is what I am doing right now, taking me towards my goals, my truth and in line with my core values or is it taking me further away? Will this choice, this action bring happiness and fulfilment or a life of mediocrity?"

Learn to make the right choices at the right time, for it is the choices and decisions in the moments of your day that will shape your future. This one question, this one process will help keep you on track more today than yesterday. It's in these moments when no one else is watching when you win or lose. Your success in all areas of life will always be determined by the choices you make and actions you take. Let go of the choices of the past, position yourself in the right environment with personal development, a coach and a mentor, and you will start to consistently make the right choices. YOU CAN DO THIS!

Have you ever wondered why some people gracefully move through life, in complete flow, and seem to effortlessly get more done? Moving forward in their career? Living a more fruitful life? Why them, rather than you and what is it they do that you seem to miss? I certainly have and still do. I am inspired by individual greatness, it gives me a desire to discover and learn what others do and have done, to live out a great life and get more done in a graceful fashion. Always be inspired by others, stop comparing and learn to mirror and model success through inspiration and association rather than competition and desperation. I am often asked "How is it Craig that you have a perfect balance between business, pleasure and adventure?" Do I? Am I graceful on the surface like a swan, yet kicking like mad beyond what you can see? I believe striking up a perfect balance of time is impossible, embracing that imperfection and giving your best in the moment is all you can do and should do, YOUR BEST.

Although being in flow and projecting this vibe sits at the foundations we have discussed in chapters 1, 2 and 3; loving what you do is enjoyable and attractive. Giving your best in your arena, positively making a difference and influencing others is also enjoyable and attractive to the eye. Remember, it's the moments of decision, that sweat equity when no one is watching, the kicking like mad under the surface that brings opportunity and reward. When you love what you do it's almost easy to follow through, you're committed rather than just interested.

So let me share with you now, how you can strike up a time balance in line with what really matters to you, however firstly you must embrace these well-known sayings:

"There is no such thing as spare time; there is always a trade-off of time to bring something new into your life."

"Short term sacrifice is always required for long term gain."

"To have what others do not have, you must be prepared to do what others will not do."

So to create financial freedom, succeed in love, life, business and creating a legacy, you must get the balance of time appropriate to your reason. In order for you to have the time and finances to do what you want, with who you love, at first you may have to spend more time doing the things you sometimes may not want to do, in order to be able to do the things you have always wanted to do.

Let me explain in the most visual way possible. I may just change the way you look at pizza forever though. However with all honesty, I could never personally be put off pizza. Interestingly if you ever want some mentoring and coaching time with me, take me to a pizza restaurant, just make sure it's a good one!

So imagine for a moment a large wall clock with the hours of time segmented like slices of your favourite pizza, stay with me on this. I believe in order for you to create total time freedom, to be able to do what you want, when you want, in the beginning you must get the balance of effort and the slices of time, even the slices of pizza appropriate and in line with your business and financial security development. This means spending more time giving value to others, often burning the midnight oil and trading off adventure and lifestyle now, in order to succeed long term. This would mean leaving less slices of time for chilling out and adventure now, and is the exact reason why working on your passion and loving what you do is so essential to enjoying the process each and every day. So in the future you have more slices of time to benefit from the fruits of your labour and live that dream lifestyle with your family and friends. I read this quote only today;

"Sooner or later, everyone sits down to a banquet of consequences."

How very true, every choice to work on your passion, every action you take will bring consequences of failure or success. The compound effect is always working either in favour of your ambitions or against them and most likely it is in line with your choice to give slices of time to your trade, your profession and your passion. Depending on your ambitions in all areas of life, be it to be an amazing partner, doting parent, athlete, successful entrepreneur, to achieve something you have yet to experience; I believe you will need to treat it like life, even like a game of poker. At some point if you want to be a winner, if you want to succeed, you have to GO ALL IN. A dedication to personal achievement is required. Are you ready to go all in? How will you use your slices of time appropriately?

With all this said, what is the secret? How do you make a change in your actions to ensure your time is used wisely and in accordance to your goals and ambitions? Responsible for 25% of your success in life is your ability to be organized. Organisation is a foundational cornerstone to your success. You can and will only go so far on pure energy and excitement, however at some point you need to be wise in your organisation.

Here's a common known saying and vibe that you will be fully aware of and know that it has affected you in life too;

"If you have all day to do something, it takes you all day."

Crazy right, yet so true!

Although most of the population fight it and even avoid admitting it, we as human beings, are creatures of habit, it's in our DNA. I would like to share with you some ideas, why they are important and how you can bring them into your day to day life. These philosophies and actions have MASSIVELY contributed to my ability to get more done, be more focused and develop the success I have over the years. Sound interesting to you?

The first step for all success is planning. Just like people plan a wedding, a family holiday, a journey, even the purchase of a new home. Behind every success and achievement lies a plan to succeed, a road map from A to B. Planning in layman terms is simply about setting tasks and producing a schedule to achieve your desired results in a set time frame.

"Planning will eliminate the chance from success. It is actually taking steps towards guaranteeing it."

Without a schedule, without clearly defined deadlines to work towards, you will simply drift along from day to day, rather than striving from opportunity to opportunity. You are a creature of habit. Every human being has the ability to write down goals and design their own future. It's what separates us from other living organisms. The reason you don't is because you are trapped by regret of the past or routine of the present. Remember, the past is for reference and now in this moment today, we shape new habits, new routines in line with your own personal blueprint for success.

Your emotional driving force, that self-motivation is the key to the kingdom. It's the key to break free from self-limiting habits and shape new clearly defined deadlines to stretch to and get more done. It's time to embrace planning for your life, though this is where you must break free from the shackles of societies mentality discussed earlier; 8 hours sleep, 8 hours work, 8 hours generally wasted. Let me share a story to get across the entrepreneurial mindset, the high achievers mindset you need to succeed.

A few years ago, a great guy joined my Network Marketing business. He was well educated yet had found himself working in a factory making bricks, working hard for someone else and being completely underpaid and under-valued. He had approached me because he was looking for an extra income after the discovery he was going to become a father. I am lucky to say, this young girl became my god daughter. However, after requiring lots of reassurance and support in getting started in the entrepreneurial world, he had done very well part time alongside his physically demanding and soul destroying job. After 6 weeks he had realised he would be financially better off handing in his notice at the factory and going full time as an entrepreneur. With the importance of his immediate financial success, it was essential we built him a strategy, tasks and schedule to succeed in his ambitions. After a lengthy discussion I asked him to transfer onto a weekly planner all we had discussed. As he proceeded to do so, the first thing he scheduled was an hour for lunch between 1 and 2pm. His first lesson appeared as I explained an entrepreneur eats when they're hungry and sleeps when they're tired. Yes, nutrition and recovery are essential fuels for you to perform, however planning in the same thinking of the job world and society will set you up for failure.

Diligence is another cornerstone of success and responsible for 25% of all you achieve, doing the right thing at the right time. Your plan should consist of revenue producing activities first, scheduled to be done at the most effective times for your business. Although always remember, an imperfect plan started today is better than a perfect plan started tomorrow. Start with what you have and better skills and abilities will be found along the way. To think 14+ years on, Richard has been one of my closest, most appreciated and trusted friends giving me the privilege to have 2 beautiful god daughters. Can I remind you;

"The quality of our life lies within the quality of our relationships."

Who would have thought all them years ago, when he gave me a look of disbelief, when I told him about this lunchtime vibe, that we'd develop into great friends? Like Richard, I have personally never achieved anything worthwhile without a specific plan of action and of course the mindset to follow through and make it happen. So here is the best way to plan, in my experience.

Everything starts with your goals and objectives; these must be in line with your passions and what's important to you. In EVERY area of life you have reference points of success where you can discover what actions you would need to take to achieve the desired result. I set my goals for the year, wherever you are in the year now, you can set you goals to finish this year strong. Then break down into step by step achievable monthly targets. This is where sitting down with and discussing with your mentor or coach has a huge importance. Then you can create weekly schedules to the end of the coming month to ensure you do what is required to hit your immediate goals and targets by the set deadline.

Make this really specific, include everything; family time, business, personal development, fitness, and coaching sessions. Your attention to detail is so important as it is the little things that can really matter. You'll be planning your success like a military operation. I will be really honest with you, this was tough for me. I am such a spontaneous character. However what I found was, with a well-defined and structured plan, I simply got more done which gave me the freedom to be my spontaneous self.

"Prior planning and preparation, prevents poor performance."

No one, including you, ever goes about doing something badly. This mindset to plan, review and work with a coach to have a fresh set of eyes will help you ensure your tasks and actions are congruent with your mission to succeed. Today is the day you change; you remove the typical old habit of going with the flow and taking it as it comes; this is a mindset of mediocrity. Spending time developing your WINNING ROUTINE is essential, however please be aware, work on yourself, work on your plan alongside the activity. Too many people stop and spend hours, even days on a plan, get it done and simultaneously keep moving. I have been doing this for over 17 years and it sits at the foundation of everything I do and is exactly what has allowed me to live the dreams I had. This mindset and strategy gives you clearly defined focus on what you should be doing.

> *"Focus on the actions of today while planning for a better tomorrow."*

As you all know life comes with its up and downs, and can often be associated to that of a rollercoaster ride. I have found over my years and have since discovered that people get bogged down with the ups and downs of life, the worry of what may or may never happen. What I have discovered is that everything you tend to worry about, everything that may bring you stress on the downs of the rollercoaster ride have actually rarely materialized; you end up just ok anyway. Something my mum shared with me many years ago when I was frustrated and felt like I was stuck, has remained with me ever since; in 6 months from now will it really matter? So often we can sweat the small stuff, allowing it to distract us from what really matters. This whole program is about stretching your mindset and removing that stinking thinking. So here's the thing, Mother Nature is built on the ups and downs of life. Consider these statements for a moment:

- The sun rises in the east and the sets in the west.
- The tide of the ocean comes in and goes out.
- The season of the year appear then disappear.

- You breathe in, you breathe out. Your chest rises and retracts.

Can you see, life itself is built on ups and downs? Embrace them, flow with them however understand this, if you focus on the depths of despair the ups and downs of life will take you there. If however you focus on fun, abundance and success, the ups and downs of life will take you there. Focus on what matters and remember:

"The strongest trees grow in the strongest winds."

It is very easy to get derailed from your plan with daily challenges and obstacles thrown your way by the winds of today. This is why a key ingredient to your success is a weekly board meeting and a weekly coaching session with your coach. Within your weekly schedule ensure you plan 1 to 2 hours a week to have your own strategic board meeting, this meeting could be as a partnership or even just you spending time on your business, fitness and life set up. What a board meeting allows you to do is celebrate your wins of the previous week and consider the lessons of personal and business growth. You can then look at the week ahead and correct and adjust accordingly to either get back on track or even get further ahead. Either way this allows you to perform at your best in the coming week and again ensuring you remain congruent to your goals.

The final piece to use your time wisely; being organised and setting yourself up for a day of high performance in all you do is working to a Daily To Do List. This one simple philosophy will change your life forever, it did mine. I was at a Leadership event back in October 2001 and a great guy was sharing his wisdom and experiences on his successful journey. One thing he said stuck with me and became the seed of empowering me to get more done; he said this;

"Never finish a day before tomorrow is on paper."

This one daily habit will revolutionise your day and your life; it is so simple and easy to do. As I said earlier sometimes it's the little things that can have the biggest impact and I believe this will for you too. All you need to do is at the end of each day create a list of everything you need to get done the following day. To create a solid to do list you focus on working from your plan and also following through from all that has come about from your actions of today. By doing a to do list every evening, you will find that the excitement and energy really does increase your productivity. Personally I have found this to be so rewarding as you tick activities off throughout the day and it also keeps you focused on what's important today, and today is the only day that truly matters. There is a science to this element of organization; by focusing on each day and writing your tasks down you will find it will have 3 major effects:

1. You will sleep better and therefore your body will focus on rest and recuperation. By brain-dumping tomorrow onto paper before you go to bed, it naturally removes the need to think about and even worry about all you need to do. It's written down and ready for you to take on tomorrow, tomorrow. Meaning, you are left with the moment of now and the ability to sleep well.

2. You will be far more proactive the following day, even finding all the excitement of today is transferred into tomorrow and not lost in your sleep. It will enable you to prioritise and focus on each task one by one, which will prevent the feeling of overwhelm.

3. In my opinion you will simply have more fun, getting more done.

   So far we have covered the Four Cornerstones of Success, each of these cornerstones represents 25% of building that end picture, confidence and belief in all you do. Alone they will impact your life, together they will change your life to that you deserve and desire. Throughout these chapters so far we have discussed:

Hard Work.

Organisation.

Diligence.

Prudence.

Now, your 'Four Cornerstones of Personal Success.'

CHAPTER 5 - BUILDING YOUR BELIEF

'Believe in yourself and all that you are. Know that there is something inside you that is greater than any obstacle'

One of the biggest challenges everyone has, is the personal belief in their own abilities. Are you good enough? Do you have what it takes and what exactly is special about you? I personally believe as I am sure you have already discovered through this book and audio program, that every one of you has the ability to achieve your heart's desire; it's in your DNA. Your beliefs are the commanders of your nervous system and sit at the foundation of every choice, action and success.

Throughout the program everything we have discussed has led us here to strengthen your beliefs. The building blocks of each section, the areas of focus and dedication will naturally build your belief and confidence. Remember these 2 one-liners I shared with you earlier;

'If someone else can, you can too.'

So often we can get lost in the fog, so to speak, falling back into the "I can't". Here's the thing though, you already are. I read a great book recently 'Who says you can't when you already do,' how so very true.

'Do the thing and gain the power.'

You will gain confidence through doing. This is why the ideas and strategies in this book are so important. They give you the foundations, the environment and even the belief that it is ok to fail, just keep failing forward. Sometimes we just have to get out of our own head, whilst we change our thinking for the greater good of living a fulfilled and present life.

So this final chapter is something that I have become very passionate about. I believe we have already walked the path of building your beliefs. Now, I would like to help you position yourself to become unstoppable and prepare you for the journey ahead, one of personal growth, challenge and reward.

From an early age we are conditioned to think, believe and act in a certain way. I would like to share with you how even at the age of 32, new beliefs and pathways to greatness can be formed.

I always believed as I grew up that I would fall in love, make a truly romantic proposal, get married and stay with that one lady for the rest of my life. A typical thought process for everyone I guess? However, as with everything, we are where we are today because of the choices and actions of the past. Some bad choices coupled with the wrong actions, lead to consequences.

Through my own experience I learnt the hard way. My relationship with the girls mum broke down, we went through some tough times. Though you know, I am blessed to still have such a lady in my life, a beautiful person and an amazing mother to my two perfect little girls. We grew apart, yet remain great friends and loving parents; that in itself is a personal belief to ensure a great environment for our girls exists.

These tough times can lead us down unknown paths, although my business, friends and family kept me busy. With all honesty I was lost and I decided to get away. I had stumbled across Reiki healing in the past having had a few treatments from a good friend of mine, and through my personal development I had developed a light understanding of how Yoga could be good for the mind, body and soul. Although a complete novice, I decided to search for somewhere abroad that I could learn both Reiki and Yoga, whilst spending some time with myself.

It was as though it was meant to be. Within minutes of searching online I had stumbled across this small retreat called 'Bann Zen' in Koh Chang, a tiny little island in the north of Thailand near the Cambodian Border.

The more I looked at it, the more attractive it became. The island, miles away from the tourist trade and Bann Zen a family home, ran by a French couple; I was massively inspired and within 30 minutes I had a trip booked just 2 weeks away. I remember packing on the day I was heading off, and a book that had recently arrived from Amazon caught my eye, so I threw it in the bag. This book I had literally purchased from Amazon as it had popped up in the 'people who purchased this also liked this' section. Its title and cover attracted me to buy it. It was 'The Biology of Belief' by Bruce H. Lipton. I am a firm believer in synchronicity and the law of attraction, though I hadn't realised how this trip would shape my beliefs, still to this day.

The trip itself, the journey, the Thai family I met and the island itself was simply beautiful. What was fascinating was how EVERYTHING connected on an Island thousands of miles away. I was learning from this wonderful lady Joy, practicing Reiki, as well as Yoga; discovering from a spiritual position how the body is formed of energy, learning about chakras, meridian lines and how to self-heal, even mediate to realign yourself. Then throughout the day, whilst relaxing on the beach I was reading this book. It blew me away. Everything I was learning spiritually was then being confirmed by science. My belief in our bodies and mind's ability to heal and achieve anything was off the scale. One of the key things I learnt was that everything is environmental, from our inside to the creation outside. How thoughts become things and understanding that the roots create the fruits. This all inspired me to contribute and was a reason why I am so passionate to help others realise their internal potential.

What is interesting about this trip, I had gone away lost, yet had discovered and found strength and developed stronger beliefs in my own ability. I really do believe we live in this society that is constantly fast paced, with people always on the go and I love this. I personally love the buzz and energy this brings. However what I found on this trip was that sometimes you need time to yourself, time to reflect and time to only worry about your own well-being.

I am a really caring and considerate person. I live my life with my heart on my sleeve and will often do more for others than they will for themselves, it's who I am. What was fascinating on this whole trip was that I never had to ask anyone what they wanted to do, how they were or if they needed anything. I selfishly indulged with myself and I have to say it was the most relaxing time I have ever had. This whole experience really made me realise that we all get lost in the day to day life, while also worrying about others.

You must have heard these certain sayings before; "to love others you must first learn to love yourself" and "you're unable to help the poor by being poor". It's along this line and the reason why I really feel you should learn to spend time with yourself, a nice walk, meditation, something for you and only you because when you connect with yourself you can really learn to connect with others too.

There is one more part of this life changing trip I would like to share with you that still makes the hairs on my arms stand up. While being on the beach, I had a massage in a family ran business. I made friends with the husband and wife. They proceeded to show me around the island. I saw things that you just wouldn't see.

One day the husband took me around one side of the island on the back of my moped and the next day his wife the other side. The wife took me to a temple up on the mountain overlooking the coastline of mainland Thailand. As it was approaching their New Year's Eve, she suggested we went into the temple. As we entered the temple, I remember you had to offer peace and gratitude and then follow a step by step regime around the Temple. This included lighting candles, randomly selecting sticks of some kind, (I am not actually sure what they were), then, when you went to the next section the result from the previous section would dictate what action you took. I hope I am making sense? Anyway throughout this 10 minute regime you are taking actions appropriate to your choices, then what presents itself to you, you take and move on. At the end of the movement around the temple, again offering gratitude at every stop, you come to a wall of scrolls and numbers. You are then given a scroll in line with what you randomly arrived with.

I have just pulled the small piece of paper from my journal that originated in the scroll, that I opened overlooking Thailand's coastline and it read as follows (It was in Thai, English and I believe Cambodian);

"Just like a dying tree, suddenly refreshed and soaked with rain, reviving back to life. Just like teenager who never knows sorrow. Legal case is favourable. Patient fast recovering. Good supports. Overall this is good."

Imagine how I felt reading that, after the purpose for my trip and all. I was learning, on the Island of Koh Chang! I believe everything happens for a reason, a lesson, personal growth or even reward.

Everything I have learnt over the years from listening to Deepak Chopra and Wayne Dyer, it all started to make sense.

"Where attention goes, energy flows."

I had listened to an audio by these two guys long before going on this trip and it was a simple conversation and phrase that I choose to believe and live by. It's your response to every situation that creates your outcome.

Dr. Wayne Dyer shared a story of a ride in a taxi and a conversation about how he never catches a cold, with the taxi driver saying "Oh, you're one of them positive thinkers." He'd simply discussed and shared how he had created a defence system, a shield even, to protect his body and that when germs land on him he had explained how his body reacts with an "I'm too strong a defence mechanism. You have landed on the wrong guy. You'll have no luck here." The taxi driver clearly thought he was crazy right, like the masses would I guess. However, this really resonated with me and changed my life.

Can I recommend you get a copy of 'How to be a no limit person' by Dr. Wayne W. Dyer and also 'How to get what you really, really want' by Dr. Wayne W. Dyer & Deepak Chopra. The impact this had shifting my belief in line with this mindset was quite astounding.

I had always had hay fever, suffering from itchy eyes and the occasional 45 minute sneezing fit. What I realised after this new found education and knowledge, was that every spring, my reaction to the grass being cut would be "Shit I'm going to start sneezing," and I would. I simply changed my belief which immediately impacted and changed my personal response. From that spring and every one since, when the grass is being cut and spring is in full swing, I breathe in the smell and enjoy knowing I now enjoy all this time of year has to offer. Guess what, no sneezing, no itchy eyes, no hay fever.

You may be wandering how this is even possible in a world of westernised medical intervention, which is in many cases lifesaving. However, I believe you have the ability to heal yourself through your thoughts and beliefs. I am aware of so many magical stories, linked into people's personal beliefs that have defied the need for drugs and medication. What's essential for you to understand is a belief is powered by you and can be changed at any time. Your beliefs of today may be different to your beliefs of tomorrow, all influenced by choice, association and new found knowledge.

Here's a common challenge and reaction for many, even you. When you walk into a room and greet someone who may have a bug, they sneeze, maybe even say "Don't come too close, you'll catch this dreadful flu" and guess what, you do, because you allow yourself to be susceptible by your beliefs.

For many years I always seemed to catch a flu bug at Christmas. I started to expect it and believe that's what was going to happen. Again after this new found knowledge, I changed my thinking, adapted my beliefs to that of; "My body is too strong and my defences repel any bugs and germs." Even, and still to this day, people say, "Don't come to close I am ill." I lean in and kiss them saying "Hello, it's ok, I'm bullet proof to germs." I have ingrained this into my children, even when I have heard other parents say this too them, I lean in and whisper in their ears, "Its ok you're too strong to catch germs." Guess what, they believe and guess what, they're never ill, well aside from the time I gave them food poisoning, however that's another story.

I dare you to challenge your beliefs, become mentally and physically stronger through shifting the way you think. I wanted to share these brief insights into a few of my experiences and how they have shaped my beliefs. I want to help you forge new empowering beliefs and a laser like focus to be the greatest version of yourself. You carry a lot of power when you understand and believe, remember;

"The strongest trees grow in the strongest winds."

In life, so many people concede to beliefs of mediocrity instead of focusing and fighting on a positive outcome. Everything I have wanted to share with you on this program and in all I do, is to show you that you have the power to be all you want to be. By positioning yourself and associating with an uplifting environment, you can become unstoppable. I would like to stress again, life is full of ups and downs, it's built into the cycle of nature. What you focus on, what you give belief and give attention to, is exactly where the ups and downs of life will show you.

Every one of you has and will continue to always look back on your journey and think you could have done better, wish you had given more, even done more. I love this, because for me this thought process shows you that if you look back and reflect in this way, which I know you do, it means you have the ability. It means you can, it shows that when you remove all the crap out of your own head, when you have a strong motive, then it shows you already believe you can. You do believe in yourself, we just need to set 'you' free opening and creating new pathways of greatness that start within.

Your beliefs are your personal blueprint for greatness; they are the birthplace of excellence. Beliefs are like the commanders of your nervous system; they are the greatest force for creating 'good' in your life. When you believe something to be true, you literally go into the state of mind of it being so. You live your daily life by your beliefs, associating feelings of pleasure and pain to every belief. It's your beliefs that will shape your destiny:

"Your beliefs become your thoughts.
Your thoughts become your words.
Your words become your actions.
Your actions become your habits.
Your habits become your values.
Your values become your destiny."

Mahatma Gandhi

The challenge you have is removing old self-limiting beliefs and choosing beliefs that will positively impact your life in the way that you desire. Everyone has both empowering and restricting beliefs. What is it that is holding you back? Do you allow these beliefs to impact your daily life?

Some self-limiting and restricting beliefs may be:

- I can't be as great as those achievers.
- That's not possible for someone like me.
- I'm not good enough.
- I can't do that. I am too old.
- I'm just always unlucky.
- I can't change.

Some empowering and life changing beliefs:

- I love challenges and will always find a solution.
- If they can then so can I.
- I can learn to achieve anything if I really want to.
- The past is the past. I will create my future.
- I choose my life's success.
- I'm as good as the best, yet no better than the rest.

It is very easy for you to confuse your beliefs with the truth; when actually, beliefs are a chosen perception that you have believed to be true. Just like my perception that gives my body strength from the germs and pollen. Although just because we believe it to be true, it may not be the case. Other people will have the opposite beliefs, and live by them each day; just like you and I.

Everyone creates a certainty around their own apparent beliefs. These truths of yours that have been ingrained over time into your subconscious mind, relatively silent and hidden away, stored in the subconscious mind, controlled by your reticulate activating system; your executive secretary. From this program you will now be aware that every belief you have, has been cultivated through your social and environmental conditioning. They have been forged by other people, shaping the way you think.

"We become what we consume."

When you understand and believe this, you can start to take responsibility for your future beliefs, shaping them to be congruent to your emotional truths, in line with your core values and heartfelt vibrations. With this knowledge you can make a shift in your philosophy to overcome every self-limiting belief with empowering uplifting beliefs.

"Beliefs themselves are choices, so you can choose at any time to change and adopt a new belief."

Like a new habit, new beliefs can be formed through attention, action and focus. The best way to form a new belief can be to gain clarity through contrast, what is the opposite of that self-limiting belief. The challenge is to replace restricting beliefs by the opposite uplifting way of thinking. Let's get proactive and start the wave of change right now, establishing a new 'I CAN' belief system.

You will see a table on the following page that allows you to document any self-limiting beliefs you may have at this time. What I would like you to do for a moment is return back to your goals, visions and emotional driving forces you established earlier on in this program. Look at what you wrote down and consider each of them for a moment. What is stopping you? What belief is holding you back for each of these goals and ambitions? I would like you to document in the table on the following page all, if any of your self-limiting beliefs that are holding you back from these passions. GO...

Self-limiting Beliefs	Empowering & Uplifting Beliefs

This is an essential process for you to follow and remove all the crap out of your mind and essentially get out of your own way to enable you to live free and on purpose. If you have skipped the section, STOP. You know my feelings on this. Do the thing and gain the strength.

Once you have completed the lists of self-limiting beliefs, it is time to move on and create the ripple of change leaving these restrictive beliefs in the past. So how do you build new beliefs, different to those of yesterday?

Well, every belief is a mental act, a cognitive behaviour. It is simply a process of acquiring knowledge through thought and experiences. It then becomes a habit where we place trust and confidence in something or even somebody. We have established that beliefs are shaped by your environment and then your perception. They have been forged by you over time; this means you can forge a new belief at any time. Like success in all areas of life, developing a new belief is neither magical nor mysterious, it's simply knowing how. You will have to be strong and decisive in your quest to forge uplifting beliefs. For example, when you are thinking as follows;

"I can't do that. I am not good enough. It's impossible."

Immediately you must command an emotional and verbal contrast and then repeat for the foreseeable future.

"I can. I can do it. I am amazing and nothing is impossible to me."

The more often you repeat this, the more you'll believe it. The stronger your conviction and emotional power, the only outcome is to believe.

What I would like you to do now is simply go back to the previous page and in the table I would like you to do the following with each of the self- limiting beliefs:

1. Read the self-limiting belief.
2. Consider for a moment the opposite empowering and uplifting belief, then write it down in the adjacent column. You must 'feel' the strength of the contrast.
3. Go back to the self-limiting belief, close your eyes and visualise the belief on a piece of paper, remove it from your mind, screw it up and throw it in the bin.
4. Draw a line through that old belief in the table.

5. Then say out loud the new empowering and uplifting belief. You must command this emotional and verbal contrast. You must 'feel' it.

6. On your next mind movie, as discussed earlier in the program, ensure these new beliefs are present. See them every day, all around you.

Once you have worked down your list, please continue to think and be aware of empowering beliefs that come to mind, document them and take the same 6 steps to forge a new belief as above. As you develop these new beliefs and strive for greatness, it is important to remember you must pay attention to your environment and who you're associating with. Be careful what you read, what you watch and what you listen to; everything matters. Be conscious on what you are allowing inside, it's your inside that creates your outside. Get around positive and ambitious people, high achievers in your field. Positive people are achievers.

"Positive thoughts and feelings are not the result, they are the cause."

Those who lead a successful life have chosen to believe in the thoughts that empower them to act. Success really is based on action and actions are the results of your beliefs. This whole program I believe, has positioned you with new found knowledge, a connection to your emotional driving force, and truly expanded your potential. Be focused on being a radiator to your own mind, remaining positive and always being solution orientated. You are the guardian to the power that lies within you. Be wise in what you consume and cultivate in your mind. Your beliefs will be the magic key to unlock your dreams and live the successful, fulfilled and happy life you deserve.

Thank you for joining me on this brief journey together through the Elastic Attitude program. Alongside what we have already been through, I would like to share some final beliefs that I believe all successful people share:s

It takes all of us to enable any one of us to succeed.
When you develop a refined appreciation for the all,
then your opportunities will start to soar.

✦ ✦ ✦ ✦ ✦ ✦

Success comes from service to others, rather than selfishness.
Give value without need of compensation. Do it because you love to.

Do it because it feels great making a difference to someone else's life.

✦ ✦ ✦ ✦ ✦ ✦

Successful people often do the things others are not willing to do.
They go the extra mile and burn the midnight oil.

✦ ✦ ✦✦ ✦ ✦

Successful people create an environment of high performance and leadership. Boldly taking on the responsibilities and commitments of creating an empowering environment and a path to success that people willingly follow.

✦ ✦ ✦ ✦ ✦ ✦

Finally I would like to thank you for joining me on this program, helping me fulfil my purpose to make a difference to others. I would like to finish this program with a great poem, one that has emotionally connected with me and so many others over my years of mentoring and coaching people to succeed.

The poem is entitled **'Never Quit**.'

When things go wrong, as they sometimes will,
When the road you're trudging seems uphill.
When funds are low and debts are high,
And you want to smile, but you have to sigh.
When care is pressing you down a bit, rest if you
must,
But NEVER QUIT.

Life is queer with its twists and turns,
As every one of us sometimes learns,
And many people turn about,
When they might have won had they stuck it out.
Never give up though the pace seems slow,
You may succeed with another blow.

Often the goal is nearer than it seems to a faint
and struggling man.
Often the struggler has given up,
When they might have captured the Victors Cup.
And they learned too late when the night came
down,
How close they were to the golden crown.
Success is Failure turned inside out,

The silver tint on the clouds of doubt.
And you can never tell how close you are,
It may be near when it seems afar.
So stick to your fight when you're hardest hit,
It's when things seem worst that
You must never QUIT.

Thank you, keep expanding your potential the world is ready for you.

Printed in Great Britain
by Amazon